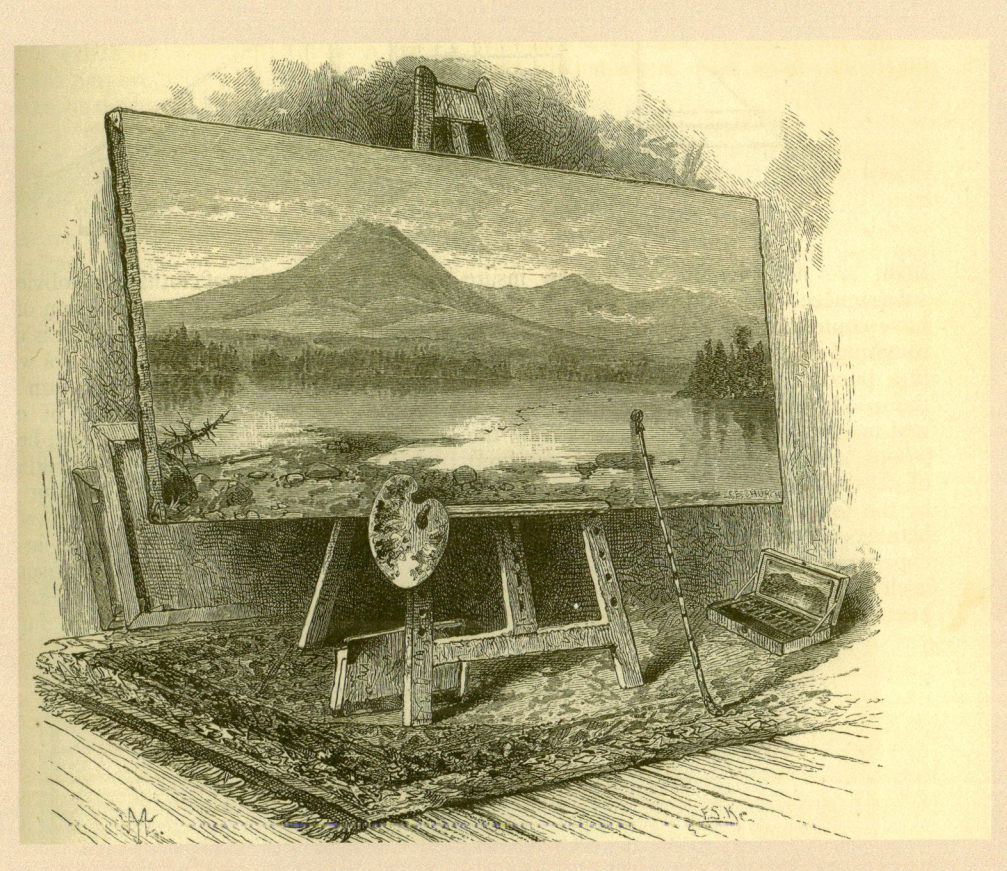

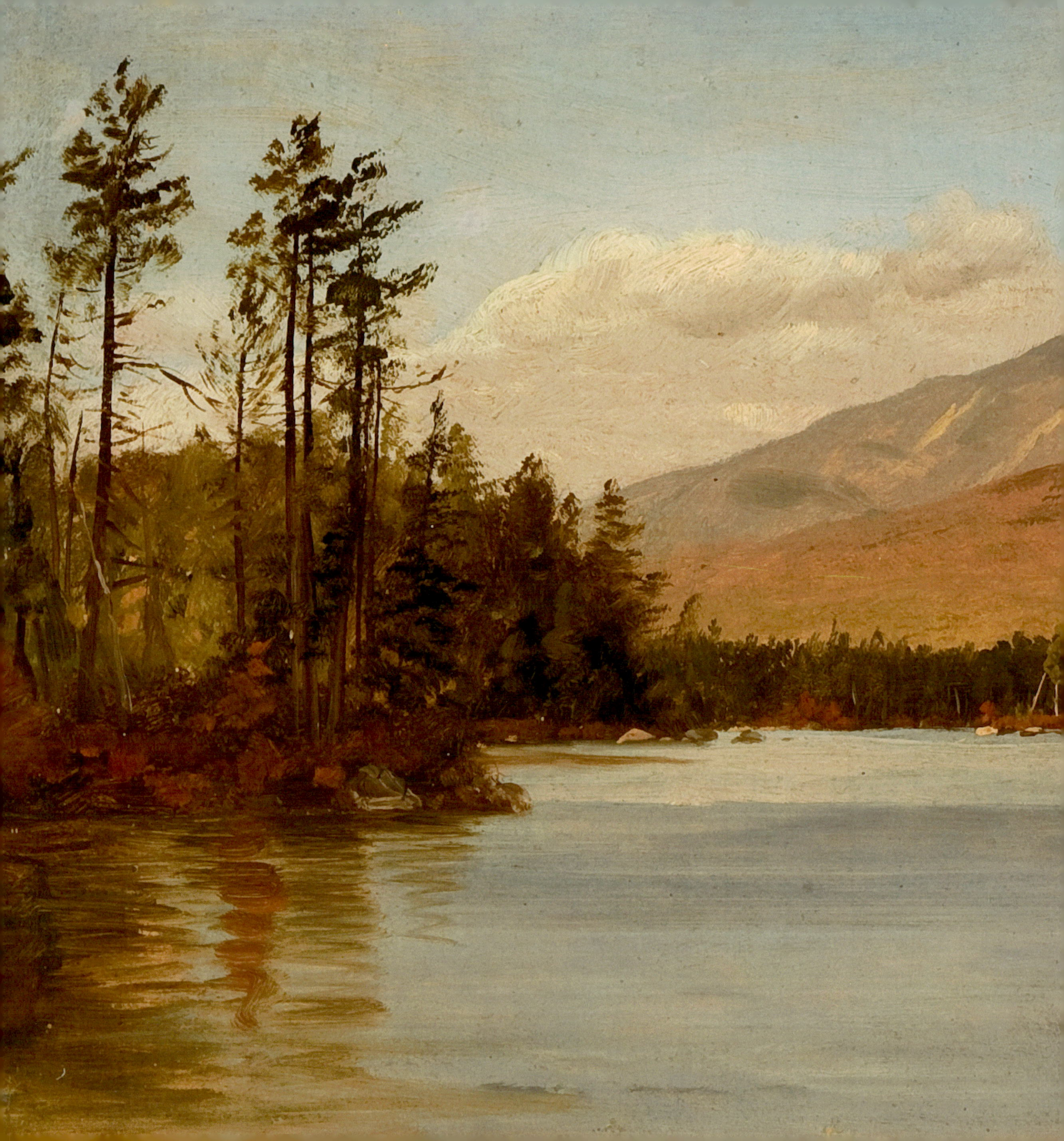

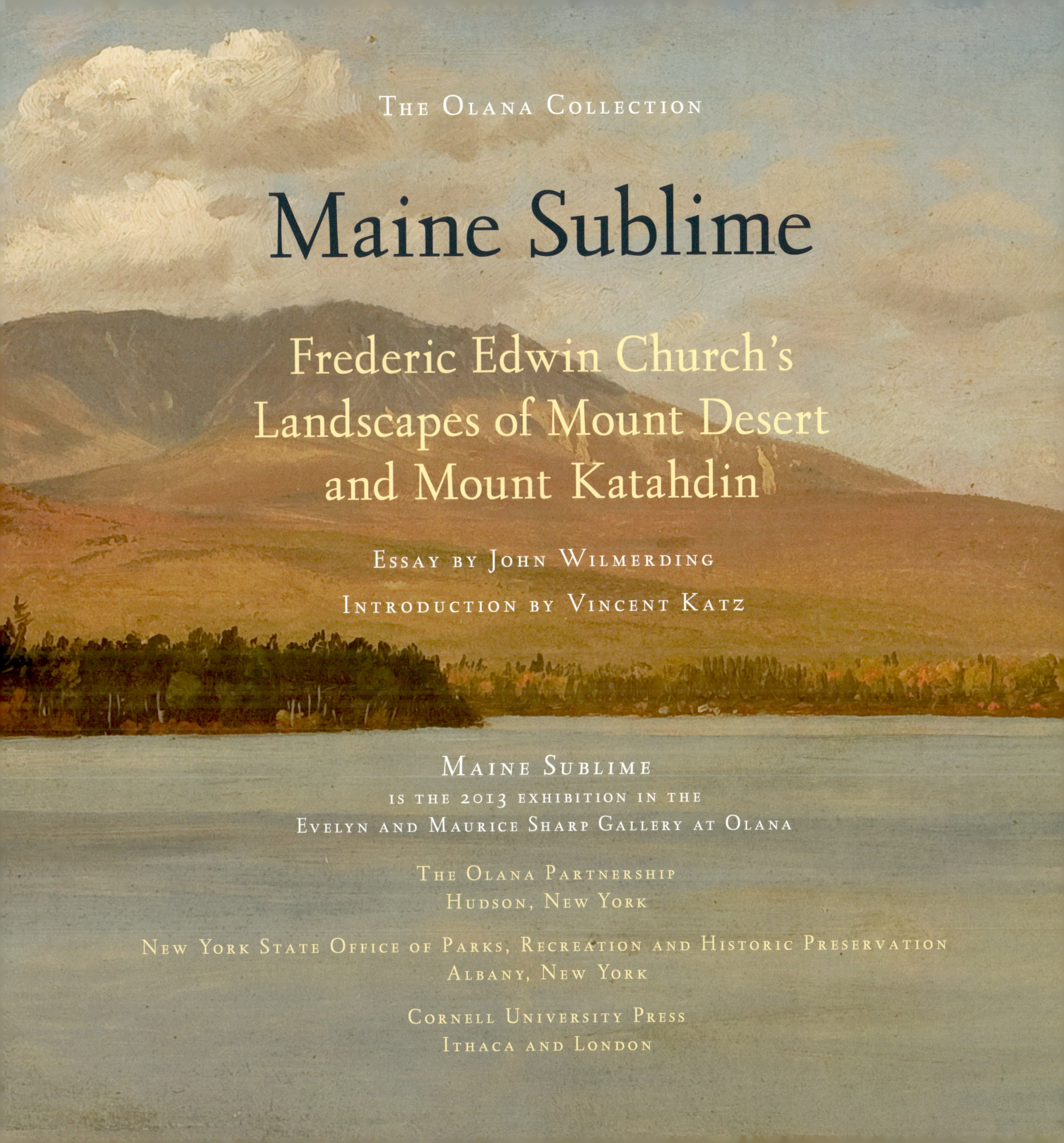

THE OLANA COLLECTION

Maine Sublime

Frederic Edwin Church's Landscapes of Mount Desert and Mount Katahdin

ESSAY BY JOHN WILMERDING

INTRODUCTION BY VINCENT KATZ

MAINE SUBLIME
IS THE 2013 EXHIBITION IN THE
EVELYN AND MAURICE SHARP GALLERY AT OLANA

THE OLANA PARTNERSHIP
HUDSON, NEW YORK

NEW YORK STATE OFFICE OF PARKS, RECREATION AND HISTORIC PRESERVATION
ALBANY, NEW YORK

CORNELL UNIVERSITY PRESS
ITHACA AND LONDON

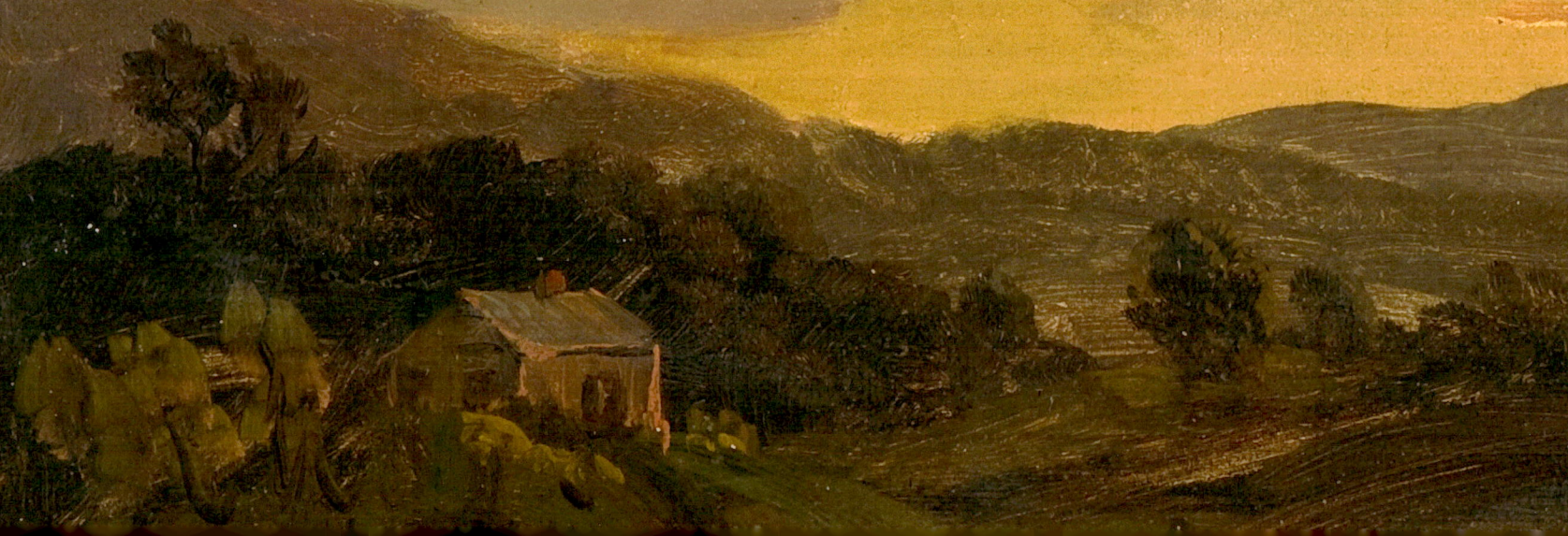

This exhibition, *Maine Sublime: Frederic Edwin Church's Landscapes of Mount Desert and Mount Katahdin*, was organized by The Olana Partnership and the New York State Office of Parks, Recreation and Historic Preservation, using objects from the collection of Olana State Historic Site, Hudson, New York.

Olana State Historic Site is one of thirty-five historic properties and six historic parks administered and operated by the New York State Office of Parks, Recreation and Historic Preservation: Andrew M. Cuomo, Governor.

Library of Congress Cataloging-in-Publication Data

    Maine sublime : Frederic Edwin Church's landscapes of Mount Desert and Mount Katahdin / essay by John Wilmerding ; introduction by Vincent Katz.
       p. cm.
    Maine Sublime is the 2013 exhibition in the Evelyn and Maurice Sharp Gallery at Olana The Olana Partnership, Hudson, New York, New York State Office of Parks, Recreation and Historic Preservation, Albany, New York.
    At head of title: The Olana collection.
    ISBN 978-0-8014-5103-4 (alk. paper)
    1. Church, Frederic Edwin, 1826–1900—Exhibitions. 2. Maine—In art—Exhibitions. I. Wilmerding, John. II. Evelyn and Maurice Sharp Gallery. III. Olana Partnership.
N6537.C4977A4 2012
759.13—dc23   2012003086

First published 2012 by The Olana Partnership and Cornell University Press. Second printing, 2014.

Unless otherwise credited, all photographs and other visual images are courtesy of Olana State Historic Site, New York State Office of Parks, Recreation and Historic Preservation.

Frontispiece: F. S. King, engraver, after Thomas Moran, "Ktaadn, from the South Shore of the Lake—From a Study by F. E. Church," from A. L. Holley, *Camps and Tramps About Ktaadn* (Scribner's Monthly Magazine, May 1878), vol. XVI, p. 33, OL.2000.438

Pages 2–3: Frederic Edwin Church, *Mount Katahdin from Upper Togue Lake*, c. 1877–78 (detail, fig. 60)

Pages 4–5: Frederic Edwin Church, *Maine Sunset*, c. 1856 (detail, fig. 41)

Page 71: Attributed to Granville Hills, *Olana from the South*, c. 1890s, cabinet card, 4¾ × 6¾ in., OL.1989.279.6

Page 72: Frederic Edwin Church, *Sunset, Bar Harbor*, c. September 1854 (fig. 39)

Page 76: Nicholas Whitman, *View from the Court Hall, south, through the Ombra, Olana*, photograph, 2001, © Nicholas Whitman, nwphoto.com

Produced by Marquand Books, Inc., Seattle
  www.marquand.com

Edited by Elaine Koss
Proofread by Carrie Wicks
Designed by John Hubbard
Typeset by Marie Weiler
Color management by iocolor, Seattle
Printed and bound in China by Artron Color Printing Co. Inc.

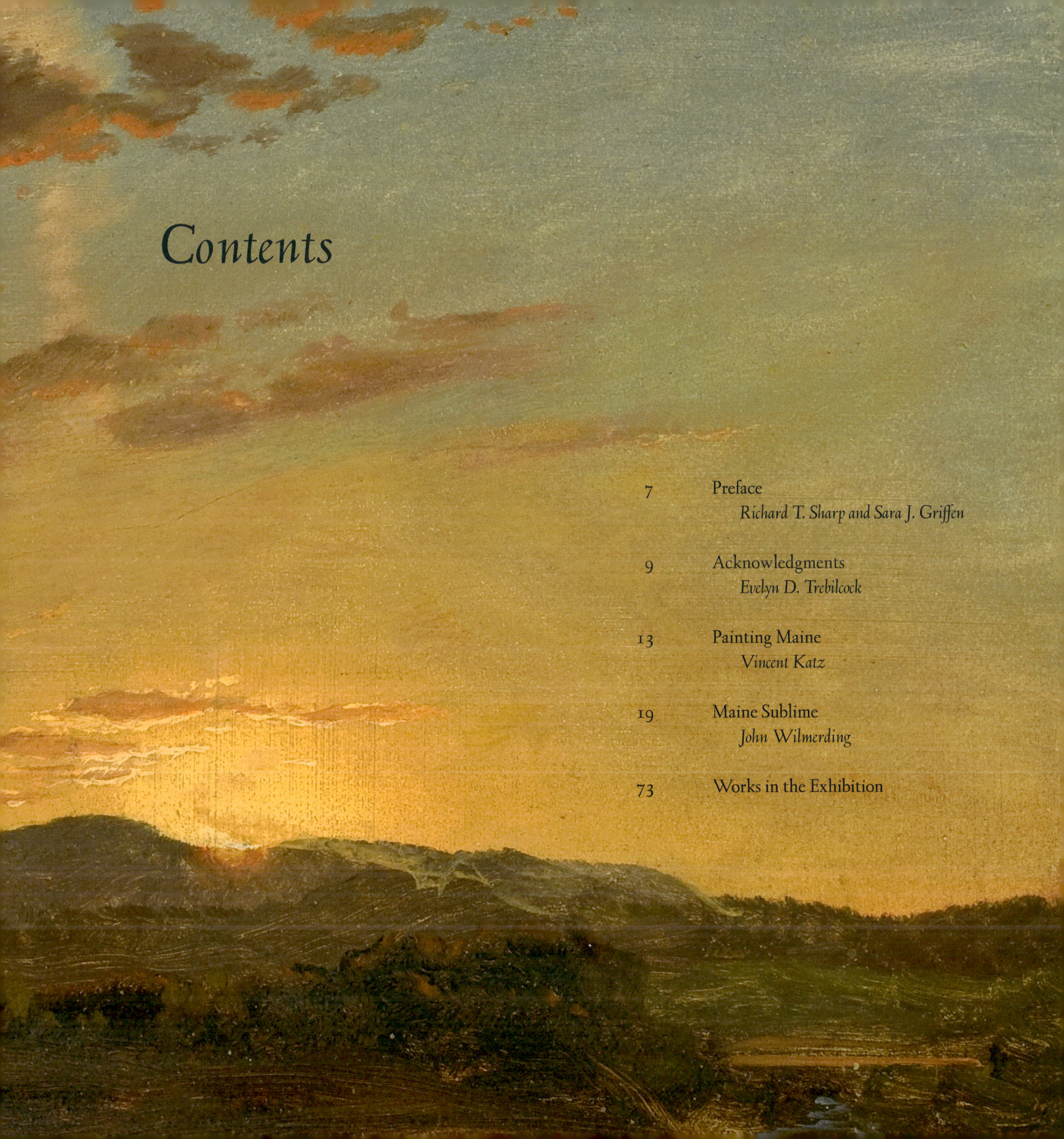

Contents

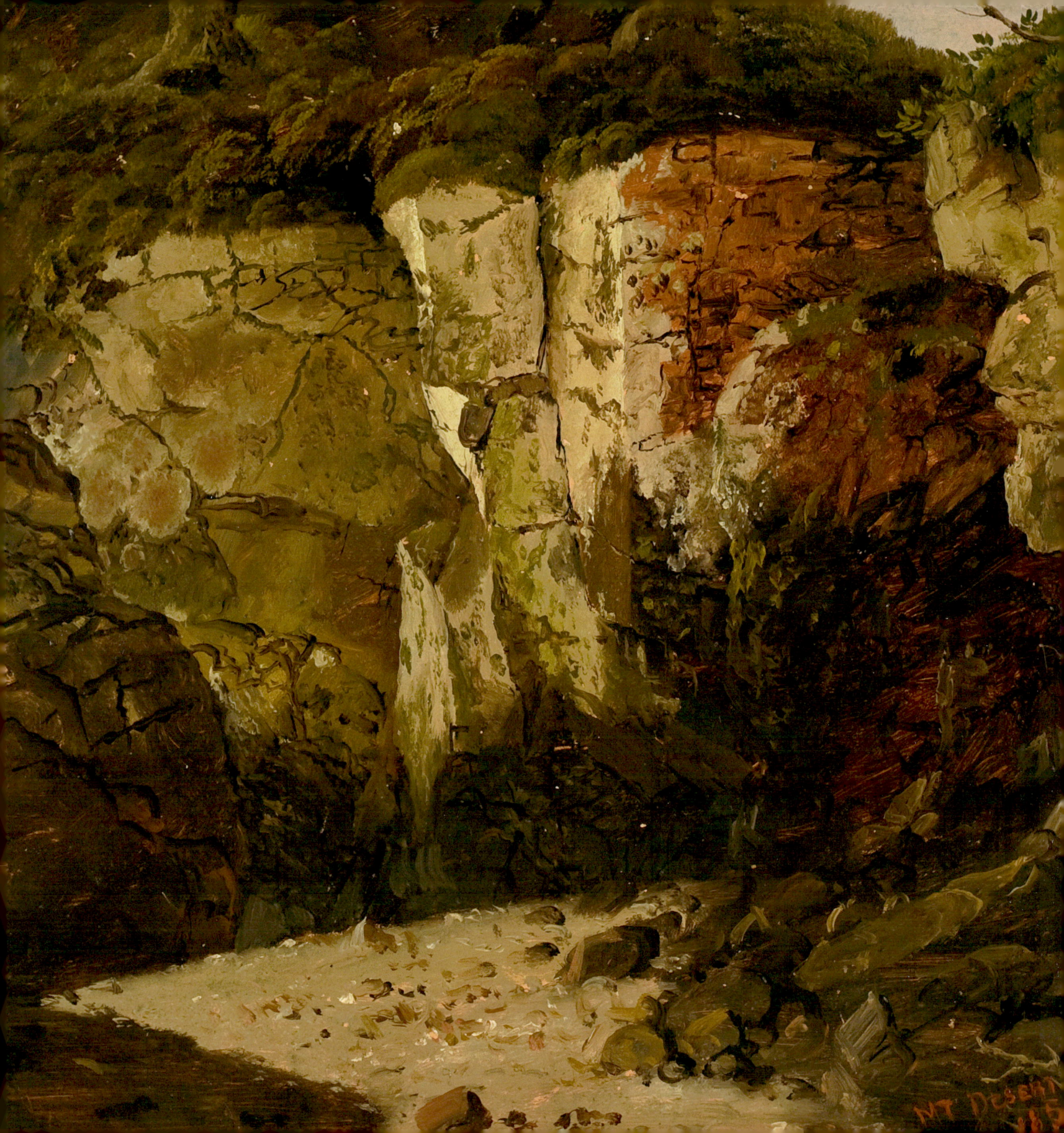

Preface

Olana's first traveling exhibition, *Treasures from Olana*, presented a selection of Frederic Church's greatest works from Olana's collection. The exhibition was hosted in 2006 by the Portland Museum of Art. To celebrate that event, a group of Olana Board members and supporters visited the exhibition and spent the weekend exploring the glorious Maine coast, focusing on the areas painted by Church, as well as by Homer and the Wyeths.

We began at Winslow Homer's studio in Prout's Neck, gazing toward the sea from his porch, walking along the rocky edge, and comparing the vista to images of his paintings. Traveling north up the coast to Tenants Harbor, we reveled in the scenery of the midcoast region so deftly captured by Andrew and Jamie Wyeth. We climbed around Jamie's lighthouse on Southern Island, where he shared with us his personal thoughts on how Maine continues to inspire his art. We then traveled north by water to Rockland, changing our perspective and admiring the rugged shoreline from the sea.

The next stop on our journey was Mount Desert Island, a place Church first visited in 1850 and described as "magnificent both land and seaward." On this leg of our adventure, we were privileged to have John Wilmerding as our guide and narrator. Beginning on Cadillac Mountain, we enjoyed a bird's-eye view of the island and the terrain that Church explored. John oriented us to the island, pointing northeast to the Porcupine Islands and west to Eagle Lake, areas Church hiked and sketched. We then

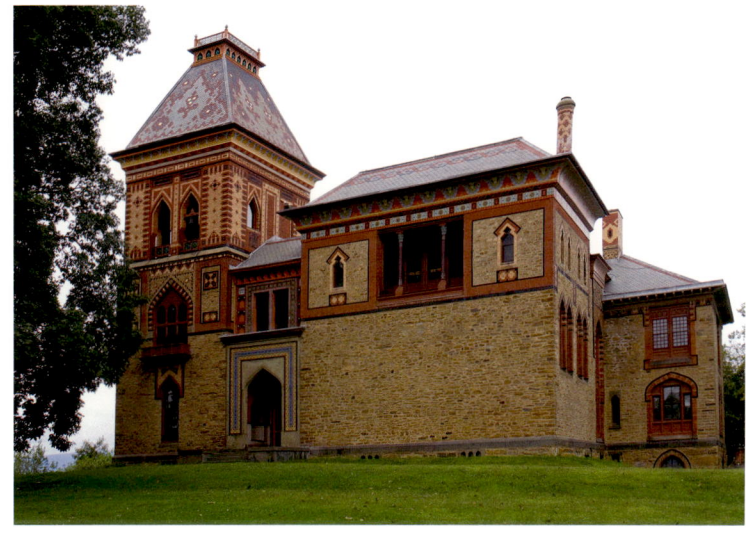

Nicolas Whitman, *East façade main house, Olana*. Photograph, 2008. © Nicholas Whitman, nwphoto.com

Frederic Edwin Church, *Cliffs and Rocky Cove, Mount Desert Island*, c. August 1850, detail, fig. 10

followed the artist's trail south along the coast to Sand Beach, where Church captured the cove and the profile of Newport Mountain, and then around the cliffs of Otter Point, which provided the material for some of Church's intricate rock studies (see fig. 9). We dined for lunch at the historic Jordan Pond House Restaurant, taking the opportunity to see the forest area preserved by Acadia National Park. John reminded us of the nature studies, *Evergreen Trees* (see fig. 16) and *Birch Tree Struck by Lightning* (see fig. 17), that Church made on his woodlands walks.

That afternoon, we again toured by boat, departing from Northeast Harbor Dock. Our destination was south along the coast and through the Narrows to Somes Sound and Somes Harbor, where Church stayed during his 1854 visit. On board, John compared the prospects we passed to Church's drawing of the area, including the lovely pencil and gouache sketch *Peninsula in Somes Sound* (see fig. 19) and the shoreline reminiscent of *Cliffs and Rocky Cove* (see fig. 10). During the evening in Bar Harbor, we were quite taken by the amazing twilight skies as vivid and breathtaking as Church's *Sunset, Bar Harbor* (see fig. 39), a perfect ending to our day on Church's Mount Desert.

As our journey came to a close, John told us about his idea for an exhibition focused on Church and Maine. As we listened to him tell Church's story and connect the sketches to the locations we had seen, we knew John's vision had to be shared with a broader audience. Church spent four decades discovering Maine, painting both the coastal scenery of Mount Desert and the inland wilderness of Lake Millinocket and Mount Katahdin. These works form a major portion of his oeuvre. The Olana Partnership is delighted to present John's knowledge and insights about these works through the exhibition and publication *Maine Sublime*.

It is through exhibitions like these that we gain an ever richer understanding of Frederic Church as a traveler, observer, and artist. This is central to The Olana Partnership's mission to educate the public about Church's genius, through his melding of art, architecture, landscape, farm, and views into what many call his greatest work of art, Olana.

Richard T. Sharp
Chairman
The Olana Partnership

Sara J. Griffen
President
The Olana Partnership

Acknowledgments

Maine Sublime: Frederic Edwin Church's Landscapes of Mount Desert and Mount Katahdin, the fifth exhibition in the Evelyn and Maurice Sharp Gallery, reflects Olana's continued commitment to enhancing Olana and Church scholarship and increasing public access to the Olana collection. In 2009 the creation of the Sharp Family Gallery, a space for the study and contemplation of Church's artworks and the many treasures he gathered, brings new drawings, paintings, and objects to viewers each year. Maine Sublime follows that tradition, presenting oil and pencil sketches spanning four decades of Church's career, many on display for the first time.

John Wilmerding's essay brings new light to Frederic Church's exploration of Maine, and the impact of the rocky coast, quiet harbors, and inland peaks on one of America's leading landscape painters. It was an honor to work with him as guest curator for this exhibition. We appreciate Vincent Katz's thoughtful Introduction, placing Church in the continuum of artists inspired by the scenery and industry of Maine and exploring their various stylistic changes.

This exhibition and the accompanying book would not have been possible without the dedication and hard work of so many of Olana's friends and benefactors. We recognize the support of this exhibition and catalogue by New York State Governor Andrew M. Cuomo; New York State Office of Parks, Recreation and Historic Preservation Commissioner Rose Harvey; Deputy Commissioner for Historic Preservation Ruth Pierpont; Regional Director, Taconic Region, Linda Cooper; and at Olana State Historic Site, former Site Manager Linda E. McLean, and Site Manager Kimberly Flook. We are also grateful to The Olana Partnership Chairman Richard T. Sharp and staff members: President Sara J. Griffen; Associate Curator Valerie A. Balint and Librarian/Archivist Ida Brier for their assistance in researching and coordinating the exhibition with the aid of Curatorial Interns Ashley Hopkins Benton and Corinne Smith; former Vice President for Development Robert Burns; Development Associate Melanie Hasbrook; and Executive Assistant Mary Curran.

The exhibition as presented in the Sharp Family Gallery is greatly enriched by generous loans from a private collection; Henry and Sharon Martin; the Portland Museum of Art, Maine; and the National Gallery of Art, Washington, D.C. For their assistance with these loans, we would like to express our appreciation to John Wilmerding; Franklin Kelly, Deputy Director and Chief Curator at the National Gallery of Art, Washington, D.C.; and anonymous.

For managing the loans and preparing the paintings, photographs, and printed material for display and photographic materials for this publication, we are grateful to the New York State Office of Parks, Recreation and Historic Preservation Peebles Island Resource Center staff: Director for the Bureau of Historic Sites John Lovell; former Collections Manager Anne Ricard Cassidy; Collections Manager Ronna Dixson and Assistant Collections Manager Mary Zaremski; Curator Susan Walker and Assistant Curator Amanda Massie; Paintings Conservator Mary Beteljewski; Paper Conservator Michele Phillips; Frames Conservator Eric Price; and Photographer Richard Claus. For preparing the Sharp Family Gallery, we thank Robert Hills. We are grateful to Suzanne Smeaton and Eli Wilner & Co., New York, for generously providing three wonderful replica frames.

The catalogue, which will serve to enlighten readers long after the exhibition closes, would not have been possible without early support from Henry and Sharon Martin and the guidance of Ed Marquand and his staff at Marquand Books. For their continued support of Olana publications, we are grateful to Cornell University Press, especially John Ackerman and his staff. We acknowledge Elaine Koss for her thoughtful editing of the essays and careful attention to the proofs.

For supporting images, we thank Loie and Alex Acevedo at Alexander Gallery, New York; Jackie Maman at The Art Institute of Chicago; Jennifer Belt and Kerry Gaertner at Art Resource, New York; Nancy Kuhl at The Beinecke Rare Book and Manuscript Library, Yale University, New Haven; Kajette Bloomfield and Adrian Gibbs at The Bridgeman Art Library; Tara Cedarholm; Jonathan Nolting at Cincinnati Art Museum; Elizabeth Saluk at The Cleveland Museum of Art; Damien Cacciolo, Gail Davidson, Greg Herringshaw, Chul R. Kim, and Jacquelann Killian at the Cooper-Hewitt, National Design Museum, Smithsonian Institution, New York; Cindy Mackey at Currier Museum of Art, Manchester, New Hampshire; Martina Curtin; Christine Caradazzo, Ryan Rothman, and Erica Stoller at Esto Photographics, Inc.; Mrs. Francis W. Hatch; Eric Baumgartner and Shelley Farmer at Hirschl & Adler Galleries, New York; Henry and Sharon Martin; Lorelei Eurto at Munson-Williams-Proctor Arts Institute, Utica, New York; Sara. Martinez-Sarandeses at Museo Thyssen-Bornemisza, Madrid; Alex Katz; Vincent Katz; Katie Kerr at the Museum of Fine Arts, Boston; Barbara C. G. Wood at the National Gallery of Art,

Washington, D.C.; Christine Bertoni at Peabody Essex Museum, Salem, Massachusetts; Private Collection (3); Brenna Cothran at The Parthenon Museum, Nashville; Erin Damon at the Portland Museum of Art, Maine; Laura Hegal at the Santa Barbara Museum of Art; Martha Small; Kelly Agnew, Erin Monroe, and Allen Phillips at the Wadsworth Atheneum Museum of Art, Hartford; Danielle Wu at the Mildred Lane Kemper Art Museum, Washington University, St. Louis, Missouri; John Wilmerding; and Kathleen Mylen-Coulombe at Yale University Art Gallery, New Haven. For contemporary images of Olana included here, we thank photographers Peter Aaron, Larry Lederman, and Nicholas Whitman.

It is with pleasure that we share these exquisite Maine images with new audiences as the exhibition travels to the Portland Museum of Art, Maine and The Museum of Fine Arts, Houston. The tour also provides the opportunity for some of the participating museums to contextualize Maine masterpieces by Church in their own collection. We would like to express our appreciation to the staffs at these institutions for making this possible, in particular Mark Bessire, Director, Thomas Denenberg, former Deputy Director and Chief Curator, and Susan Danly, Senior Curator, Portland Museum of Art and Gary Tinterow, Director, Emily Ballew Neff, American Painting and Sculpture Curator, The Museum of Fine Arts, Houston.

For their advice and encouragement of the exhibition and this publication, we want to recognize the Olana Curatorial Committee: Susan Winokur, Chair; Armin B. Allen; Will Cotton; Stephen Edidin, Chief Curator, New-York Historical Society; Barry Harwood, Curator of Decorative Arts, Brooklyn Museum; Mary Ellen Hern; Judith Hernstadt; Frederick D. Hill; Bindy Kaye; Paul Leach; John Lovell, Peebles Island Resource Center; Chas A. Miller III; Amy G. Poster, Curator Emerita of Asian Art, Brooklyn Museum; Richard T. Sharp; Carol Irish Strone, Carol Strone Art Advisory; and Karen Zukowski, Independent Scholar.

Finally, we wish to thank the generous individual and institutional donors that provided the necessary funds that have made this important book and exhibition possible: Valerie and Brock Ganeles; The Mr. and Mrs. Raymond J. Horowitz Foundation for the Arts, Inc.; Mark LaSalle; Henry and Sharon Martin; the New York State Council on the Arts Museum Program; The Olana Partnership Exhibition Fund; The Olana Partnership's Jack Warner Fund for Creativity and Innovation; Gary Schiro and Robert Burns; The Peter Jay Sharp Foundation; John Wilmerding; Barrie and Deedee Wigmore; Susan Winokur and Paul Leach; and the Wyeth Foundation for American Art.

Evelyn D. Trebilcock
Curator, The Olana Partnership

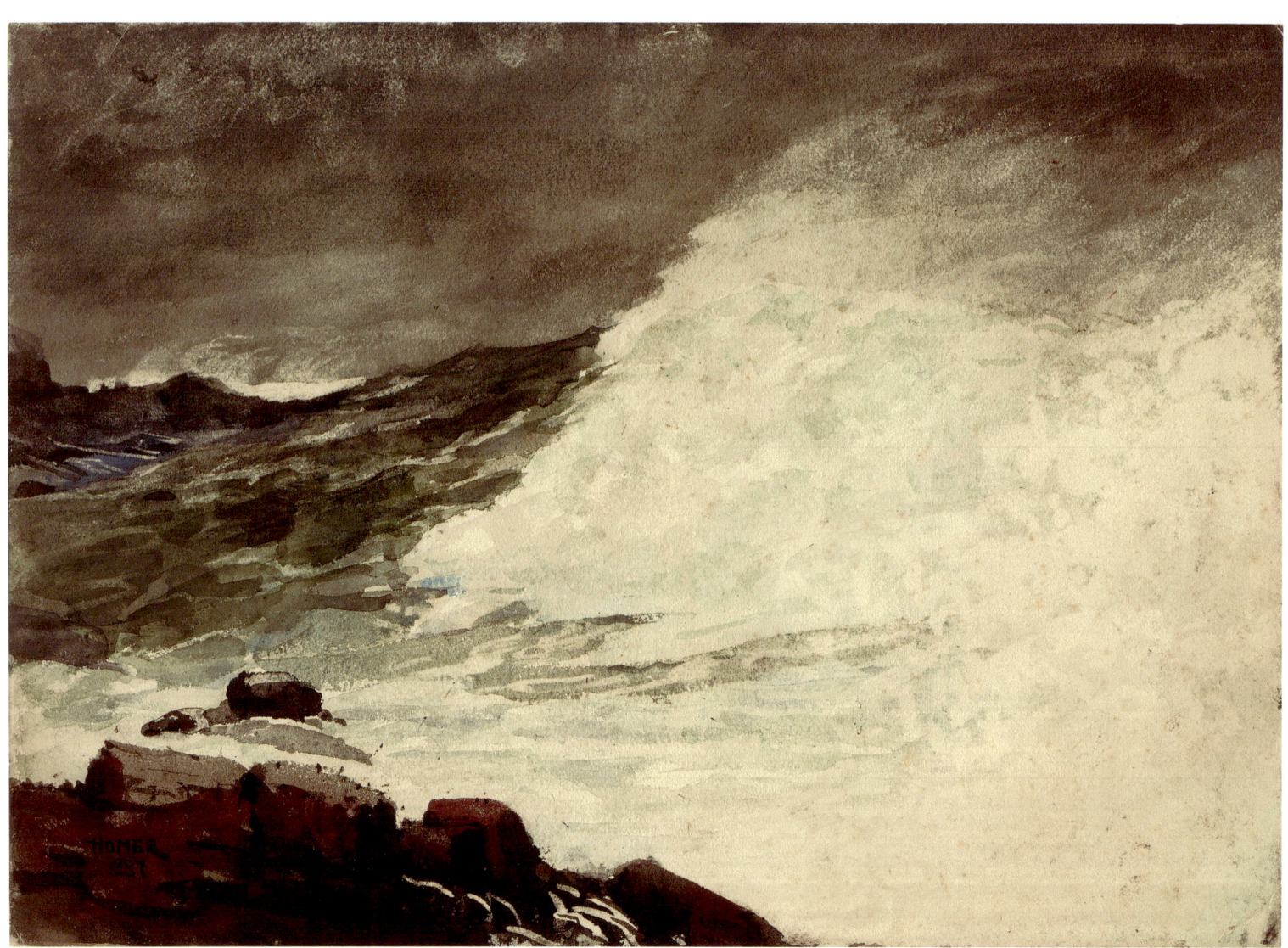

Vincent Katz

Painting Maine:
A Look at Artists' Interpretations
of the Maine Landscape

People have always been drawn to the region now known as Maine. They have been summoned by Maine's natural beauty, its verdant lushness—even in winter—its clear light, and its plentiful fauna, both on land and in the waters. Regarding painting, and in relation to thinking about Frederic Edwin Church's paintings of Maine, it is worthwhile to compare some approaches that followed his. In terms of subject matter, style, and technique, later painters tackled the Maine experience with a variety of approaches, incorporating innovations of their times or making innovations themselves.

Winslow Homer (1836–1910) was based, for the last twenty-seven years of his life, at Prout's Neck, Maine, where he created enduring images of northern waves pounding massive boulders. Whereas Church was more drawn to the open serenity of Maine's inland skies, Homer attempted to fix in paint moments in the midst of terrific explosions of energy at the coast. The coast itself is symbolic of the border between relative stability and the dangerously pulsating, unfixed, rhythms of the places one must go in order to survive, to earn one's living, and in a larger sense to move to the next phase in life. Homer's images contain this symbolism, and his way of painting conveys those borderline emotions.

Some of Homer's Maine seascapes possess airs reminiscent of Church's depictions. In both Church's oil on paper *Sunset, Bar Harbor*, 1854 (see fig. 39), and Homer's 1894 watercolor *Breaking Storm, Coast of Maine* (The Art Institute of Chicago), an area at the lower right of the image portrays a calm extension of the water's plane, reflecting dying afternoon sunlight, which has the effect of bathing that plane in a light-hued monochrome. The point of view of the observer in each is slightly different—that of the Church is more elevated—but there is an even greater difference in the emotional tone of each painting. Where the Church is painted with his characteristic delicate precision, the Homer has a wildness to the depiction that suits the meaning of the piece, which is the

Fig. I. Winslow Homer, *Prout's Neck, Breaking Wave*, 1887, transparent watercolor with touches of opaque watercolor, rewetting blotting and scraping over resist and traces of graphite on medium weight, moderately textured, ivory wove paper laid down on cream wove paper, 15 × 21½ in., The Art Institute of Chicago, Mr. and Mrs. Martin A. Ryerson Collection, 1933.1248. Photography © The Art Institute of Chicago

calm before the storm. Homer's attraction to instability goes much farther than even that example. He reveled in the actual bounding crash of the ocean, as evinced in his 1887 watercolor *Prout's Neck, Breaking Wave* (fig. 1). Here, he devotes the entire right-hand portion of his image to the foaming wave, and the result is remarkable, considering that watercolor, despite its name, is quite a dry technique. Oil paint is a medium more conducive to portraying water, and Homer made good use of it as well. He gives a foothold at the lower left of *Prout's Neck, Breaking Wave*, where he uses a more precise line to describe boulders lining the shore, in contrast to the rewet, blotted, and scraped surface of the gargantuan waves and imposing gray sky.

One can discern a link between Homer's paintings of the Maine coast and those of Edward Hopper (1882–1967), mainly in the way each man characterized the juncture of sea and land, with its implications for men whose livelihoods depended on assaying the hazardous deep. Whereas Homer tends to be more narrative, giving the viewer details of fishermen's travails and dangers, Hopper is more concerned with painterly effects, in attempts to convey the light, air, and surfaces of the rocks and grasses he sees. Later, Hopper develops a metaphoric level to his work, particularly in his series, done in the late 1920s, of watercolors and oil paintings of Maine lighthouses, in which the difficulties of living on the sea are alluded to, while the formal elements effected by his cropped views of vernacular architecture give his work a distinctly modern tone.

Marsden Hartley (1877–1943) was not drawn to Maine. Rather, he was born there, in Lewiston, and during the first decade of the twentieth century devoted part of each year to painting there. His life and career were spent alternately denying and embracing this heritage. In the 1910s, he worked mainly in Germany and France, and in an essay written in 1918 he stated, "Something must take the place of the America, of New England, in all our ways, esthetically speaking." Like many artists of his generation, he went to New Mexico, and then he went back to Europe. In the late 1920s, he returned to New England, where he complained of the "commercialism of the nouveau riche. . . . I shall be happy enough to get out of New England never to enter it again." Yet, finally, in 1937, he decided to return to Maine to live, and he was based there for the rest of his years. It could be argued that he painted some of his most significant works during this time, taking inspiration not only from coastal life but also from the woods and lives of those in the interior of the state.

Unlike his contemporary John Marin (1870–1953), also long associated with Maine, who used the landscape more as a ground for modernist compositions, Hartley sought the cataclysmic stories of the common man testing his strength against the elements. In *Northern Seascape, Off the Banks*, 1936–37 (Milwaukee Art Museum), which Hartley painted in Nova Scotia just before moving back to Maine, the principal subject is the battering of waves on shore rocks. He makes these waves into physical objects, at least as solid as the rocks. Solid, too, are the great triangular clouds in the sky, outlined in white. Hartley seems to be equating these natural elements of wave, rock, and cloud, endowing them all with stability, while man is dwarfed, his presence represented by two sailboats, small in comparison to the natural elements and caught between them, with only a narrow path to ply between wave-battered rocks and heavy, descending clouds. Many of his Maine seascapes present the sea in similarly elemental terms.

Hartley reveled in the strangeness, too, of the regional experience in Maine. *Abundance*, 1939–40 (fig. II), is an odd image. A picture of logs being floated down a river, it has an almost geometric, two-dimensional, abstract effect. And yet, in the brutal economic realism of the place and time, Hartley creates an unexpected image of wood as plenty, as nourishment.

Fairfield Porter (1907–1975) came from the Midwest, but his family had ties to Maine and in fact owned a small island, Great Spruce Head Island, in Penobscot Bay. The siblings shared the island, with Fairfield's family inheriting the Big House his father had built. Over the years, Porter painted many defining images at Great Spruce Head Island. He painted trails and paths on the island, but he is most known for sun-soaked images of the Maine grasses and conifers leading down to seaweed-laden rocks. One can almost smell the air in these paintings. Another type of painting he did in Maine is reminiscent of work he did at his winter home in Southampton, Long Island. In these works, Porter painted family and friends inside the Big House, often on the screened-in porch, where he was able to expand upon the fascinating senses of interior and exterior he admired in the paintings of Édouard Vuillard.

In this brief survey, we have been able to see how different generations of artists responded to Maine, using their own versions of the art of their time to reinterpret familiar visual elements. Hartley's 1941 painting of Mount Katahdin (Hirshhorn Museum and Sculpture Garden, Smithsonian Institution, Washington, D.C.), for instance, is much more cropped than Church's expansive vistas (see figs. 60 and 66), and Hartley treats the landmass as a hulking darkness, as distinct from Church's more nuanced tonal approach. Porter, influenced by Vuillard's use of

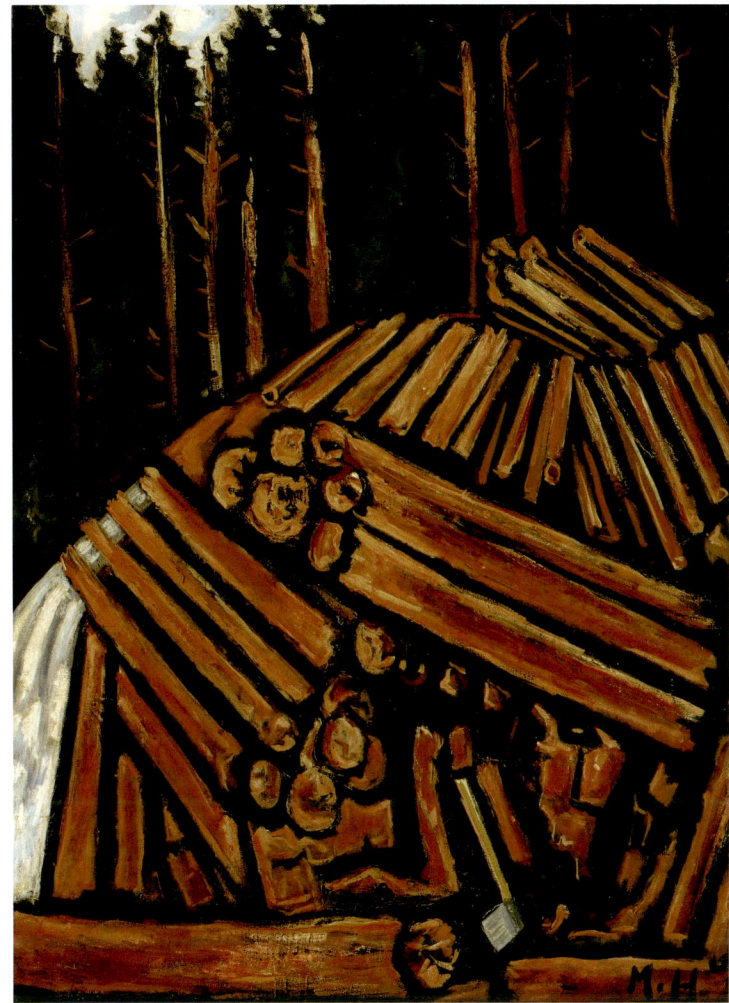

Fig. II. Marsden Hartley, *Abundance*, 1939–40, oil on canvas, 40⅛ × 30 in., Currier Museum of Art, Manchester, New Hampshire, Museum Purchase: Currier Funds, 1959.2. Photograph: Jeffrey Nintzel

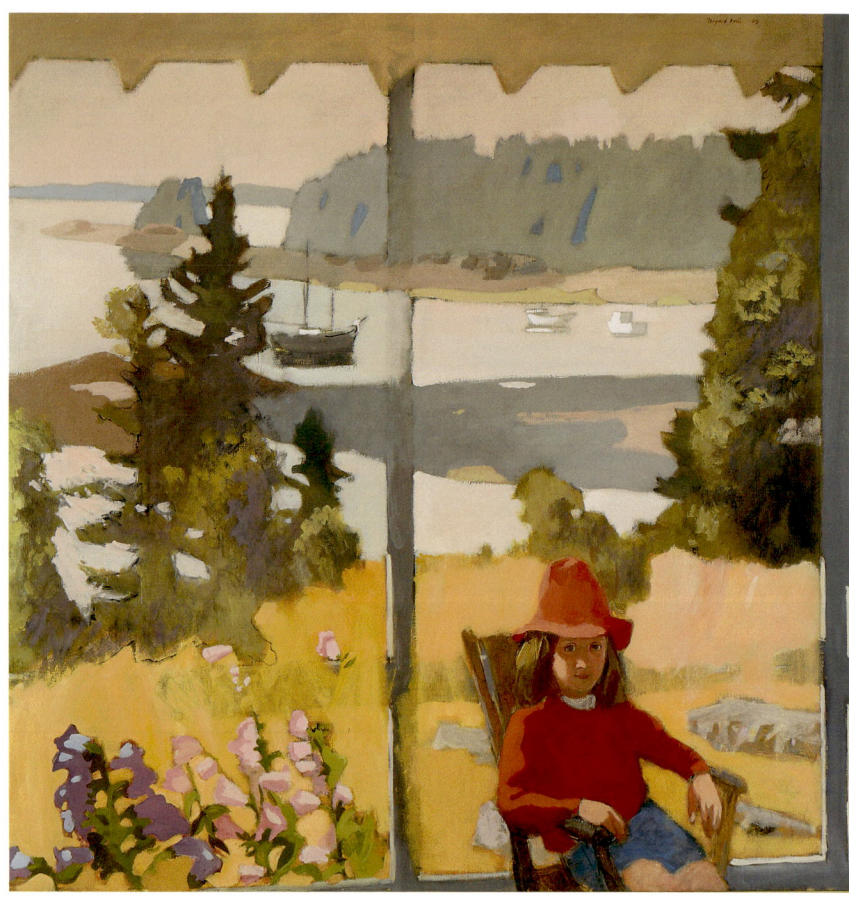

Fig. III. Fairfield Porter, *Morning Landscape*, 1965, oil on canvas, 79½ × 80 in., Santa Barbara Museum of Art, Gift of Rowe Giesen, 1991.87.1. Photograph: Scott McClain

static marks within realistic compositions, as well as by Willem de Kooning's powerful dynamics of paint handling, attempted to meld these approaches in images that were intentionally familial and domestic (fig. III). Alex Katz also responded to earlier artists' achievements and expanded on them in his images of Maine (fig. IV).

Katz (b. 1927) first went to Maine as a student at the Skowhegan School of Painting and Sculpture in 1949, and it was then that he discovered his predilection for direct painting from life. While he would later transfer this type of painting to urban subjects, he began in the countryside in Maine, and he continues to this day to spend every summer there, in Lincolnville, looking for new ways to envision the landscape. Techniques for renewing the idea of landscape have included the turbulent use of visible brushstrokes in the early work, details of clothing, buildings, furniture, and cars that pinpoint a contemporary time and place, and, since the 1980s, large-scale paintings that wrap around the viewer, creating what the artist calls "environmental" paintings. Another important element, underlying all of these, is an appreciation and use of abstraction, whether it be a solid bank of color, standing in for a sky, or a field of flowers whose all-over energy was inspired by the paintings of Jackson Pollock.

Lois Dodd (b. 1927) began spending summers in Lincolnville in 1954, later buying a place in Cushing, and she has come back to Maine every summer since. Her Maine paintings, including close-up views of windows of farmhouses, doubling as mirrors, and moonlit landscapes, have gained acclaim for their individual vision.

Many other artists have come to Maine since and worked with its particular landscape as subject matter. Neil Welliver (1929–2005) was born in Pennsylvania and moved to Lincolnville, becoming identified with the state because of his paintings of the Maine woods. He chose to use artificial-seeming colors, claiming that he was not interested in painting from nature. While his paint handling often seems perfunctory, his imagery is personal. Rudy Burckhardt (1914–1999) bought a house in Montville, not far from Lincolnville, joining the growing artists' enclave there. His first summer in the Lincolnville area, Burckhardt rented a house with his wife, the painter Yvonne Jacquette (b. 1934), the poet and critic Edwin Denby (1903–1983), and painters Red

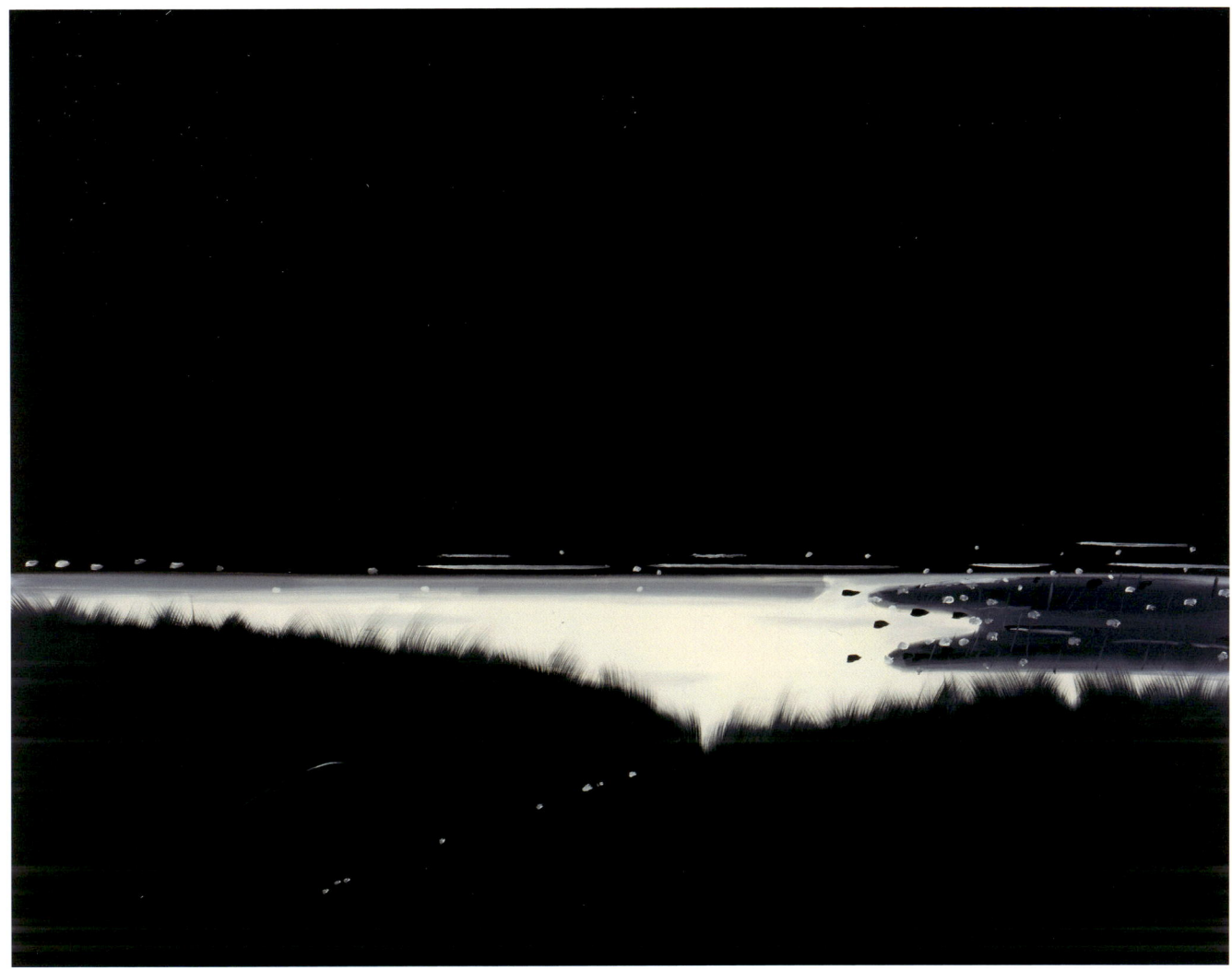

Fig. IV. Alex Katz, *Coleman Pond 3*, 1995, oil on linen, 96 × 126 in., collection of the artist

Grooms (b. 1937) and Mimi Gross (b. 1940). That summer, 1964, they all collaborated on a film entitled *Lurk*, based on the novel *Frankenstein*. Further summers resulted in further film collaborations, often with visiting poet, dancer, and painter friends, photographs and paintings by Burckhardt, and Jacquette's developing explorations of aerial views, many of them done by renting small planes and flying over local towns. Painter Rackstraw Downes (b. 1939) had a place not far from Lincolnville in the 1970s, and it was there that he began to develop his defining wide-angle format, as well as a taste for subjects such as that portrayed in his 1986 painting *Dragon Cement Plant, Thomaston, Me.: The Rock-Crushing Operation* (United Missouri Bank Collection). We have come a long way from Church's Romantic visions of a pristine nature surrounding Mount Katahdin; surely artists in the future will find other ways of representing Maine's singular vistas.

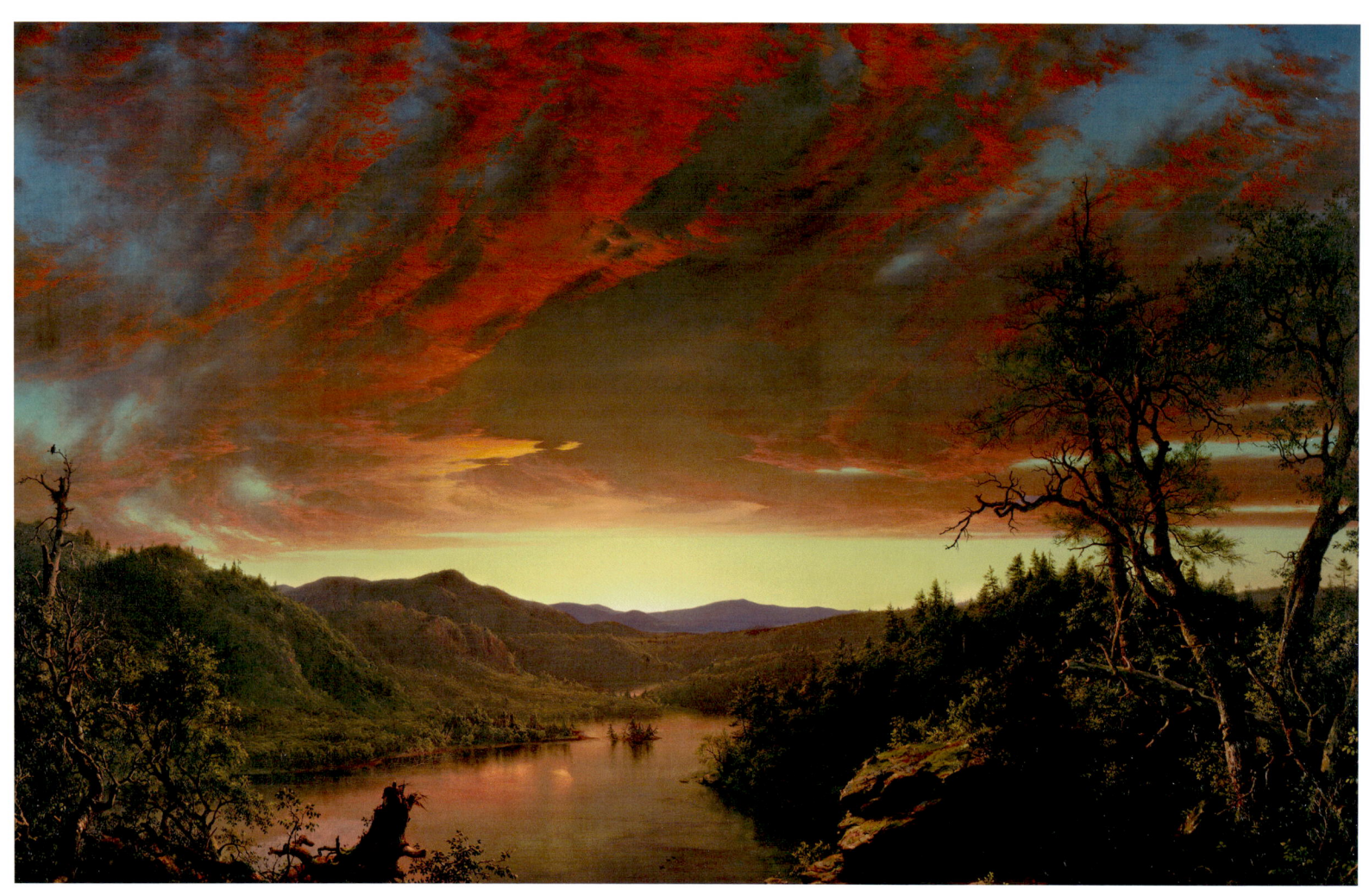

John Wilmerding

Maine Sublime:
Frederic Edwin Church's Landscapes of
Mount Desert and Mount Katahdin

Wenow recognize Frederic Church (1826–1900) as one of America's great artists of the nineteenth century. Further, many believe his work done in Maine includes some of his most important images, with *Twilight in the Wilderness*, 1860 (fig. 1), based on a sunset he had seen and sketched at Bar Harbor a few years earlier, ranking among the dozen greatest paintings in the history of American art.

Church was a public and a private artist. His paintings address both history and autobiography. The work done in Maine during the 1850s and early 1860s, primarily at Mount Desert, embodied sentiments of increasing national strife, in symbolic and suggestive ways, while the career of the later 1860s and 1870s was devoted more to his personal time in inland Maine around Mount Katahdin. Where his earlier production was extroverted and exclamatory, the later was often nostalgic and withdrawn.

How Church came to travel to Maine is embedded in the years of his youth and initial artistic training. His biography is now well documented: born in 1826 in Hartford, Connecticut, of an old New England family, he showed an early talent for drawing. This soon led his father to consult with Daniel Wadsworth, the prominent local collector of American pictures by the foremost landscape artist of the day, Thomas Cole (1801–1848), and founder of the Wadsworth Atheneum. Church senior asked Wadsworth to intercede with Cole, then at the peak of his maturity and influence as the leader of the Hudson River School of painting, to take the teenaged Church on as an apprentice, the only formal student he would ever have. From 1844 to 1846 Church entered the Cole household in Catskill, New York, as pupil, assistant, companion, and occasional baby-sitter to the young Cole children.

The first summer together must have been a crucial experience for both men, for in 1844 Cole decided to make an excursion over to the Maine coast. He traveled with fellow artist Henry Cheever Pratt from Boston and made the unusual journey inland by buckboard from upstate New York, through the mountains of New Hampshire and

Fig. 1. Frederic Edwin Church, *Twilight in the Wilderness*, 1860, oil on canvas, 40 × 64 in., The Cleveland Museum of Art, Mr. and Mrs. William H. Marlatt Fund, 1965.233. Image © The Cleveland Museum of Art

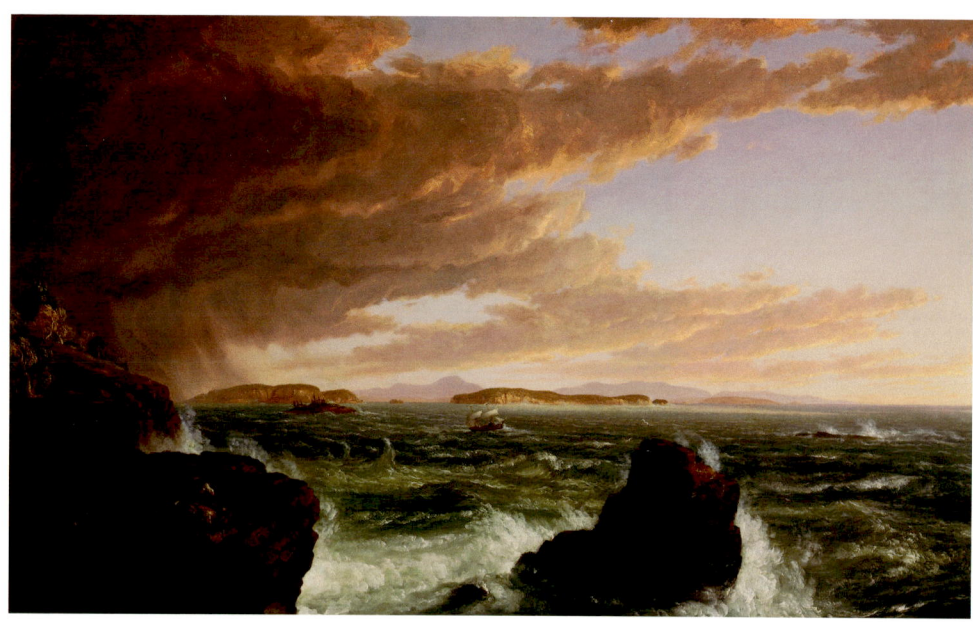

Fig. 2. Thomas Cole, *View across Frenchman's Bay from Mt. Desert Island, after a Squall*, 1845, oil on canvas, 38¼ × 62½ in., Cincinnati Art Museum, Gift of Alice Scarborough, 1925.569. Image Courtesy The Bridgeman Art Library (CIN402941)

across central Maine, finally approaching Mount Desert Island from the north via Ellsworth. (Previous adventurers like Thomas Doughty, Alvan Fisher, and Thomas Birch traveled the coast by steamer and sailing vessels.)[1] Cole kept a sketchbook, which he filled with more than a dozen pencil drawings of the surrounding area as well as panoramic views of and from the island itself. Among them were precise records of Sand Beach, the Porcupine Islands off Bar Harbor, and inland valley views, all of which Church would revisit a few years later.[2]

Imagine the apprentice's interest and excitement when Cole returned to Catskill with his sketchbook and began to paint over the next year at least three canvases based on his trip: *House, Mt. Desert, Maine*, c. 1845 (Fogg Museum, Harvard University Art Museums), *Frenchman's Bay, Mt. Desert Island, Maine*, 1845, a view of Otter Cliffs (Albany Institute of History & Art), and *View across Frenchman's Bay from Mt. Desert Island, after a Squall* (fig. 2).[3] Church was learning from Cole both how and what to paint. There were distortions and compositional adjustments in Cole's views, which he made to improve and idealize nature. As Church's style matured after Cole's death, he followed the evolving taste toward a more exacting and explicit recording of sites, but his teacher's work in that exotic coastal wilderness obviously impressed him deeply.

Two years after the apprenticeship, in 1848 Cole died prematurely, probably from tuberculosis. The young Church continued to develop his own style even as he made paintings in overt tribute to his teacher and more subtle variations of his compositions. But by 1850 Church's talents had sufficiently advanced in their technical virtuosity and imaginative choices of landscape subjects that he was clearly emerging as one of the successors to Cole in leadership of the Hudson River School. At the same time in these critical years, several other artistic and literary forces were coming to fruition that would convince Church to make his own pilgrimage to the Maine coast.

Two paintings in particular apparently had a key impact on Church, both shown at the annual exhibition of the Art-Union in 1849, to which he had submitted work of his own. Together they forecast new directions in both his subject matter and means of expression. One was a turbulent seascape by the German painter Andreas Achenbach (1815–1910), most likely *Clearing Up, Coast of Sicily*, 1847 (The Walters Art Museum, Baltimore), depicting rough waters crashing on a rocky shore.[4] The precise brushwork and dramatic lighting were typical of the currently fashionable Dusseldorf manner, which Church would rework with surpassing power and less theatrical exaggeration in his own seascapes at Mount Desert over the following decade. A subsequent review of the exhibition noted that the seascape "seems to have directed the attention of our younger men to the grandeur of Coast scenery." The reviewer went on to observe that Church was ready "to try his pencil in a new field of art."[5]

An even more influential painting on view at the Art-Union in 1849 was one sent to New York by a contemporary working in Boston, Fitz Henry Lane (1804–1865). The catalogue listed it as *Twilight on the Kennebec* (fig. 3) and added the following description: "The western sky is still glowing in the rays of the setting sun. In the foreground is a vessel lying in the shadow. The river stretches across the picture."[6] The vessel is a

Fig. 3. Fitz Henry Lane, *Twilight on the Kennebec*, 1849, oil on canvas, 20 × 30¼ in., Collection of Mrs. Francis W. Hatch, on loan to the Peabody Essex Museum, Salem, Massachusetts, M22672. Image Courtesy of the Peabody Essex Museum

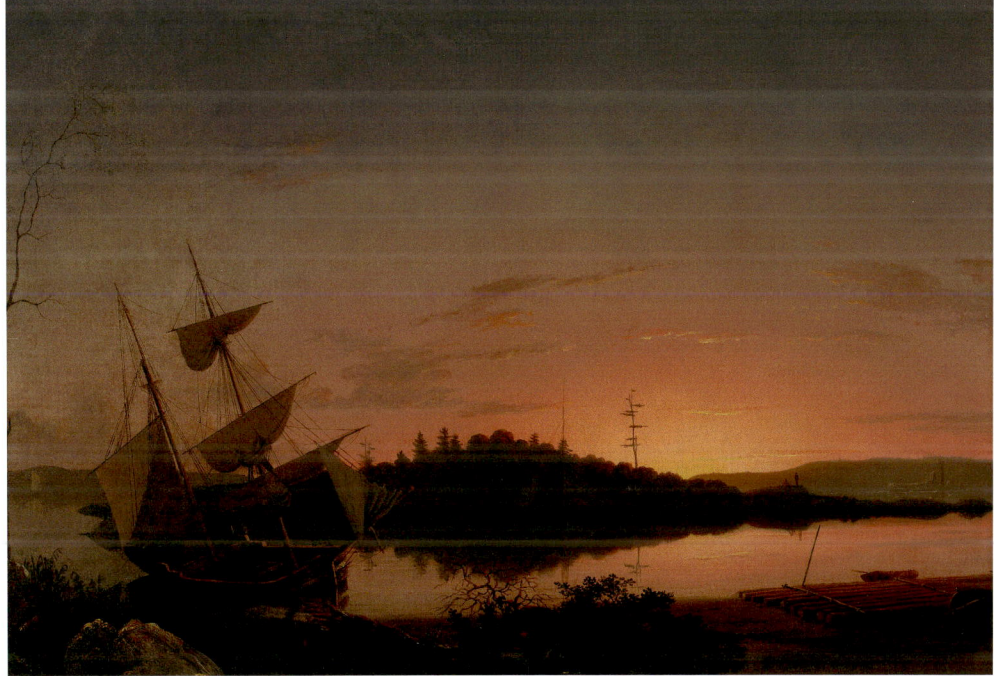

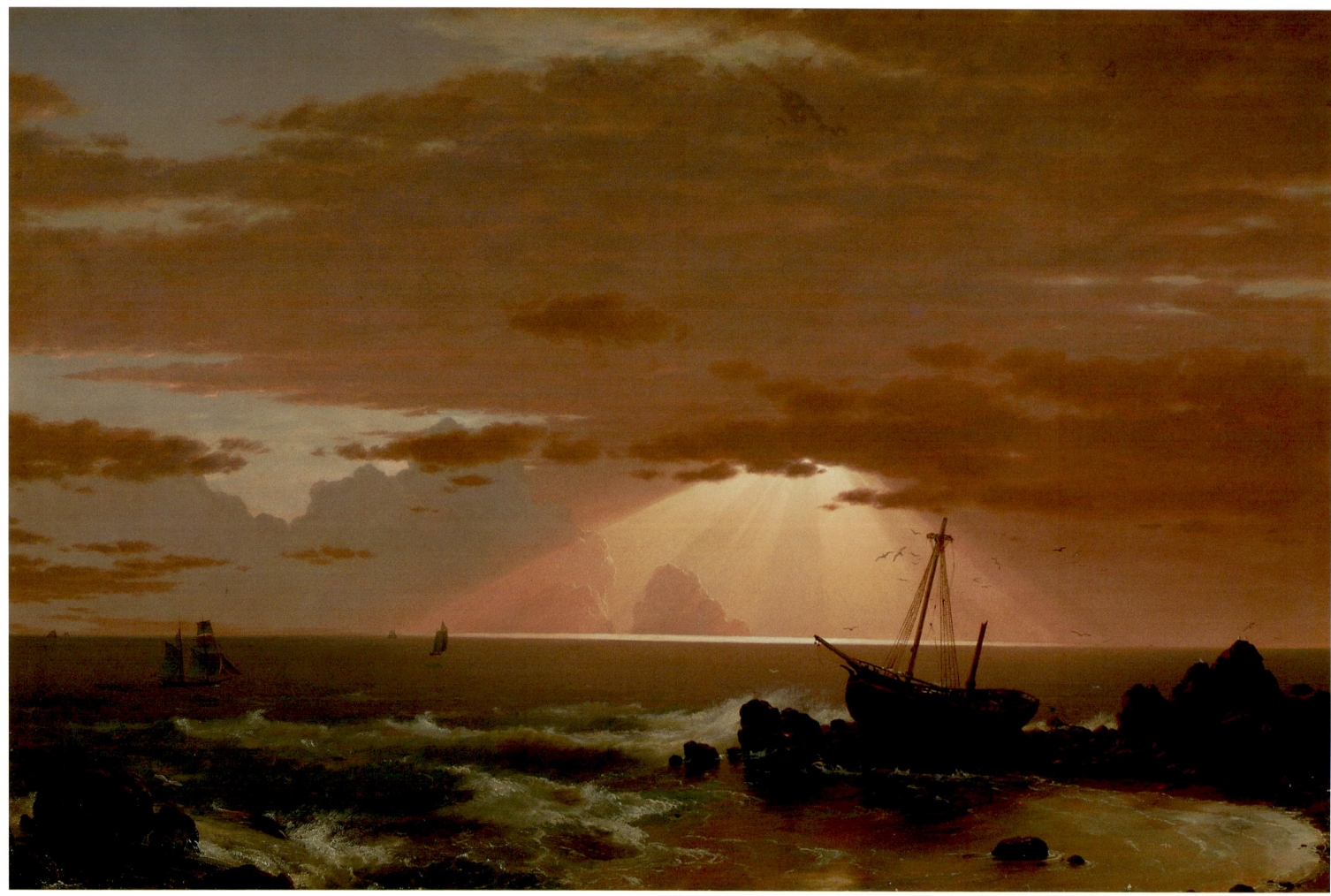

Fig. 4. Frederic Edwin Church, *The Wreck*, 1852, oil on canvas, 30 × 46 in., James M. Cowan Collection of American Art, The Parthenon, Nashville, Tennessee, 29.2.14. Image © 1929 The Parthenon

large schooner loaded with lumber, her sails hanging limply as she is grounded out on the receding tide, the wind expired for the day. This was one of the many coastwise ships engaged in the transport of wood and granite harvested in Maine for building and paving projects farther south. The image would take on a different meaning in Church's hands three years later when he painted *The Wreck* (fig. 4) at Mount Desert.

Barely visible in the right background on the river in Lane's painting is a steamer, among the first to open up passenger and freight traffic among the coastal islands and ports. The artist captures this moment of equilibrium and transition at midcentury between the age of sail and that of steam, though this economic narrative will contrast with Church's inclination toward a more scientific realism in recording wilderness nature. But the most startling and new aspect of Lane's painting to capture Church's attention is of course the radiating sunset suffusing the whole composition. As is now well known, this effect was due to the newly available cadmium pigments of reds, pinks, and orange-yellows. Not only did Church depart for the Maine coast himself the following summer, but he immediately began a series of canvases devoted to incandescent sunrises and sunsets. Many see this group painted from 1851 to 1865 as one of his signature accomplishments.

Finally, it is likely that the writing of another New Englander, Henry David Thoreau, also shaped Church's ambition to try new subjects along the coast. Thoreau's first essay on what would become *The Maine Woods* was published in 1848 in *Union Magazine* as "Ktaadin and the Maine Woods." This centered on the writer's trek into the northern Maine wilderness to climb that mile-high peak, described in the exclamatory language of the sublime. For an artist it must have sounded extraordinarily exciting and alluring. Thoreau's writing in many ways parallels Church's artistic vision in its dual celebration of nature's pastoral and awesome elements. The painter would not visit the Maine peak on his first trip, but in 1852 he followed Thoreau's example, and the experience produced one of his finest early wilderness landscapes. The vivid memories endured, as Church returned often in later years and bought property overlooking the great mountain.

Over a thirty-year period from 1850 to 1880 Church made more than a dozen trips to Maine, nearly half to Mount Desert during the 1850s and the remainder to the Katahdin region mostly in the two decades following. Thanks to the preservation of large numbers (several thousand) of his drawings and sketches by his family at Church's home Olana (now a museum) and in the Cooper-Hewitt National Design Museum in New York, we have a good idea of his prolific output. Besides his masterpieces of other subjects, such as Niagara, South America, the Mediterranean, and the Middle East, Maine commanded a major portion of his artistic time. For example, Olana holds well over one hundred drawings and oil sketches just of Maine subjects, largely from the earlier trips, whereas the Cooper-Hewitt's collection of comparable numbers is strongest in the later period.

Mount Desert is one of the largest islands on the Atlantic coast of North America, some sixty square miles, about two hundred miles northeast of Boston and one hundred from the Canadian border. It extends out into the Gulf of Maine and open Atlantic and was formed by volcanic and glacial actions in prehistory. The former pushed up the mountain ranges, followed by their gouging out during the ice age, leaving a range of hills interspersed by ponds and one five-mile fjord running from the center of the island south to open water.[7] Today the eastern and southern shores of the island display especially dramatic headlands and rocky cliffs, most of which are now incorporated into Acadia National Park. In Church's day most of the coastal reefs and ledges were unmarked, while much of the island was forested except for the growing intrusion of farms and mills. Fishing, lumbering, and quarrying soon prompted the building of wharves and lodgings in several harbors around the island.

From an account doubtless by the artist himself, entitled "Mountain Views and Coast Scenery, by a Landscape Painter" that appeared in the *Bulletin of the American Art-Union* in November 1850, we have a direct description of Church's first voyage to Mount Desert that July and August. He matched the vividness and exuberance of his words with an almost explosive production of drawings and sketches of island scenery. He took the train to Portland in southern Maine, then boarded the steamer *Governor* to Castine and sailed the last stretch on the schooner *Charles* to Seal Harbor. Church's narrative of his trip is worth quoting at length:

> We have not come thus far to be disappointed, I assure you. . . . There is an immense range of mountains running through the island, one some two thousand feet high, of admirably varied outline. . . . We are exceedingly delighted with the scenery, and with the people too.
>
> Around in Frenchman's Bay, there are precipitous rocks that come down abruptly to the water, some four hundred feet high. You face the East there; and in stormy weather, the surf dashing against the rocks must be grand. [He went on to exult about] the fierce, frolicsome march of a gigantic wave. We tried painting them, and drawing and taking notes of them, but cannot suppress a doubt that we shall neither be able to give actual motion nor roar to any we may place upon canvas.[8]

From Seal Harbor, Church could have easily walked inland to nearby Jordan Pond, where he made a drawing looking across the water to the hills beyond, *Penobscot Mountain and the Bubbles, Mount Desert Island*, 1850 (Olana State Historic Site), which led to a painting he finished the next year (fig. 5). He soon settled himself on the eastern side of the island, we believe at the Lynam farm near Schooner Head, then becoming a popular place for artists to locate. There he produced a hasty sketch of the headland, with its small cove and beach nearby and the fields inland, as well as a much more finished topographical drawing of the site. The location gave him easy access to other views along the coast and across Frenchman's Bay.

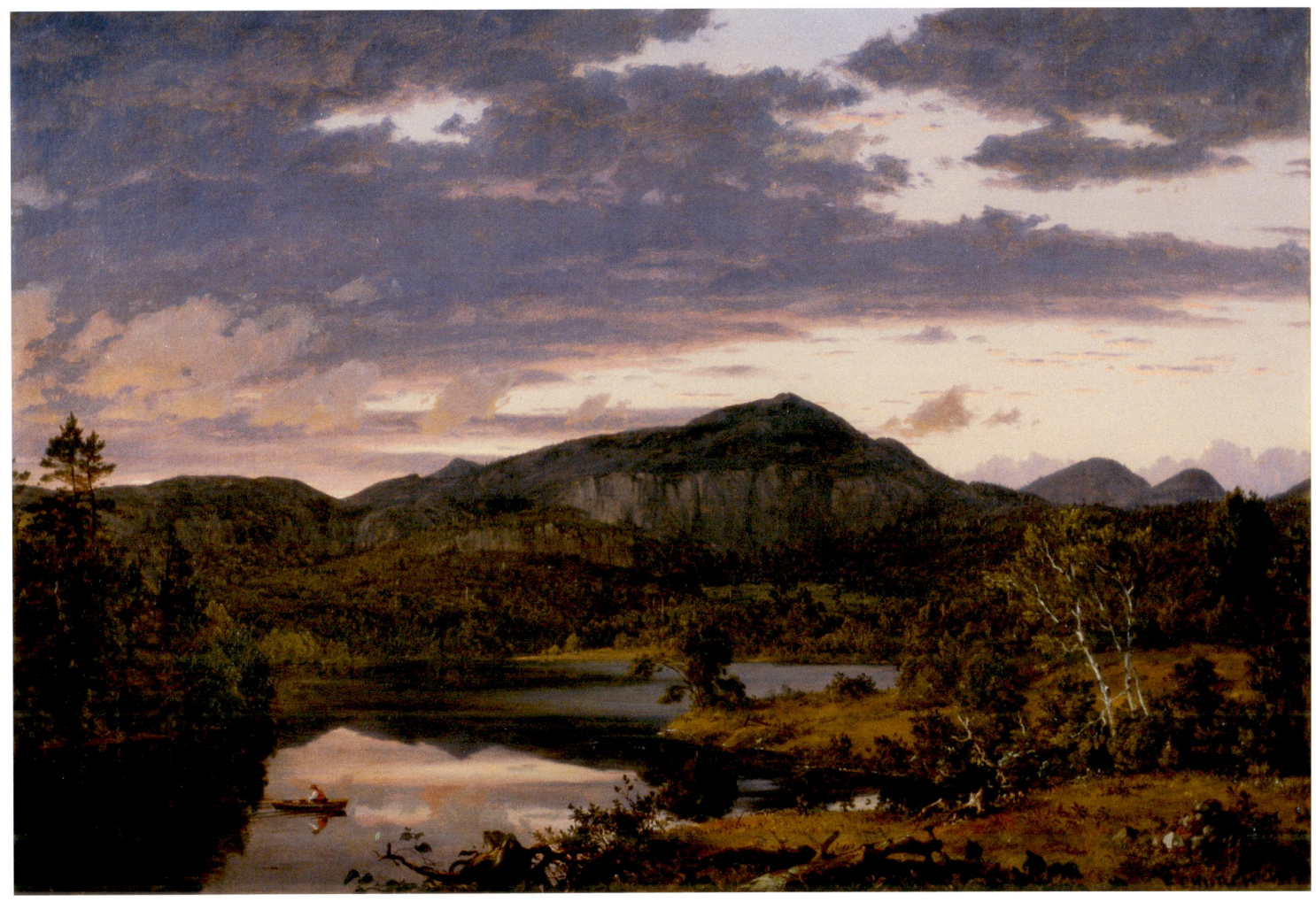

Fig. 5. Frederic Edwin Church, *Lake Scene in
Mount Desert (Little Long Pond and Jordan Cliffs)*,
1851, oil on canvas, 20¾ × 30⅞ in., Private
Collection. Image Courtesy Alexander Gallery,
New York

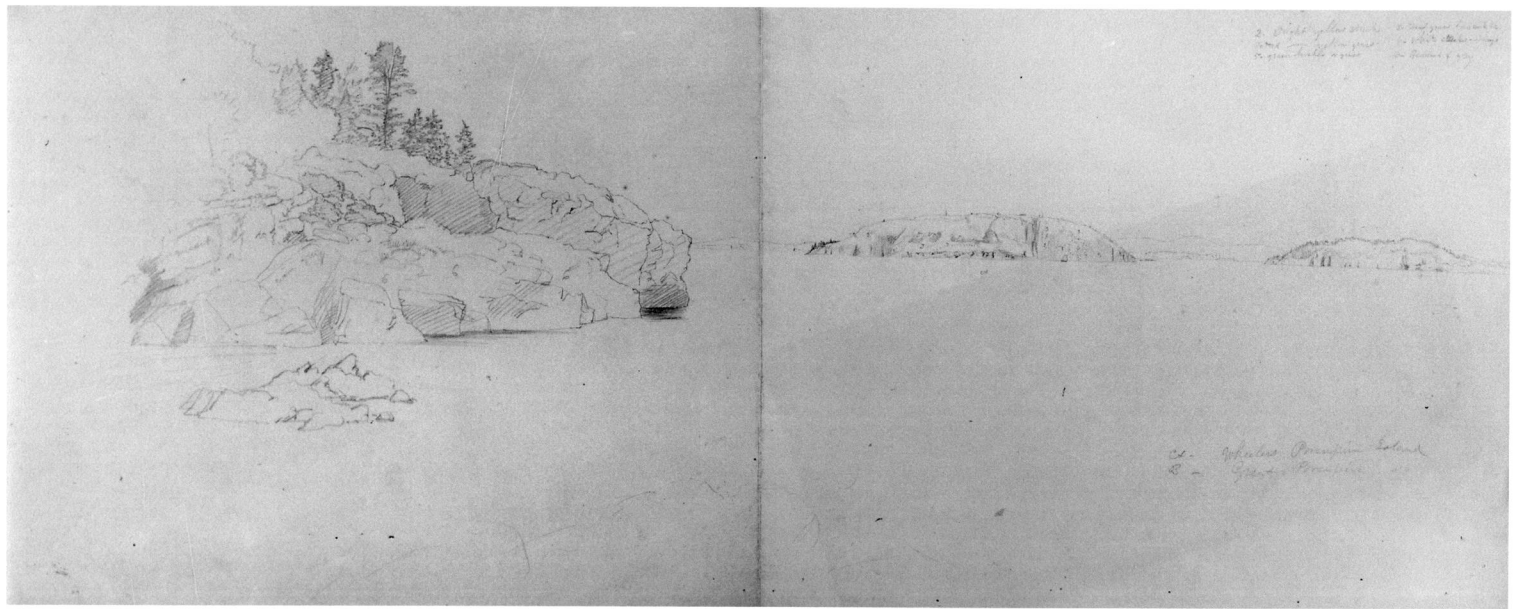

Fig. 6. Frederic Edwin Church, *Sols Cliff
and the Porcupine Islands, Mount Desert Island*,
September 12, 1850, graphite on buff paper,
9⅞ × 25³⁄₁₆ in., OL.1977.110

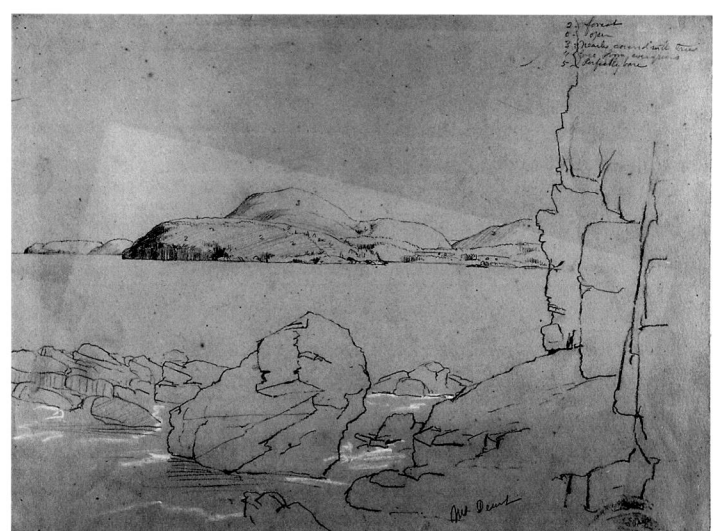

Fig. 7. Frederic Edwin Church, *Mount Desert
Island from Bald Porcupine Island*, August 1850,
graphite on light tan paper, 10¾ × 15¹⁄₁₆ in.,
OL.1980.1446 verso

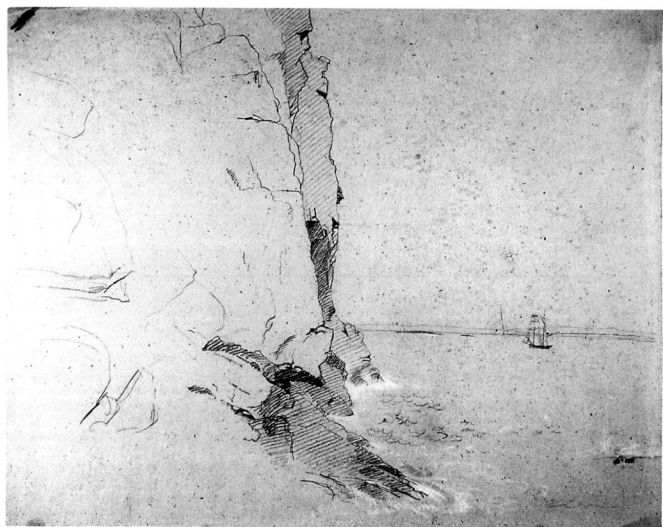

Fig. 8. Frederic Edwin Church, *Cliffs on One of
the Porcupine Islands*, c. August 1850, graphite
and gouache on coarse light brown paper,
11¼ × 14⁹⁄₁₆ in., OL.1980.1462

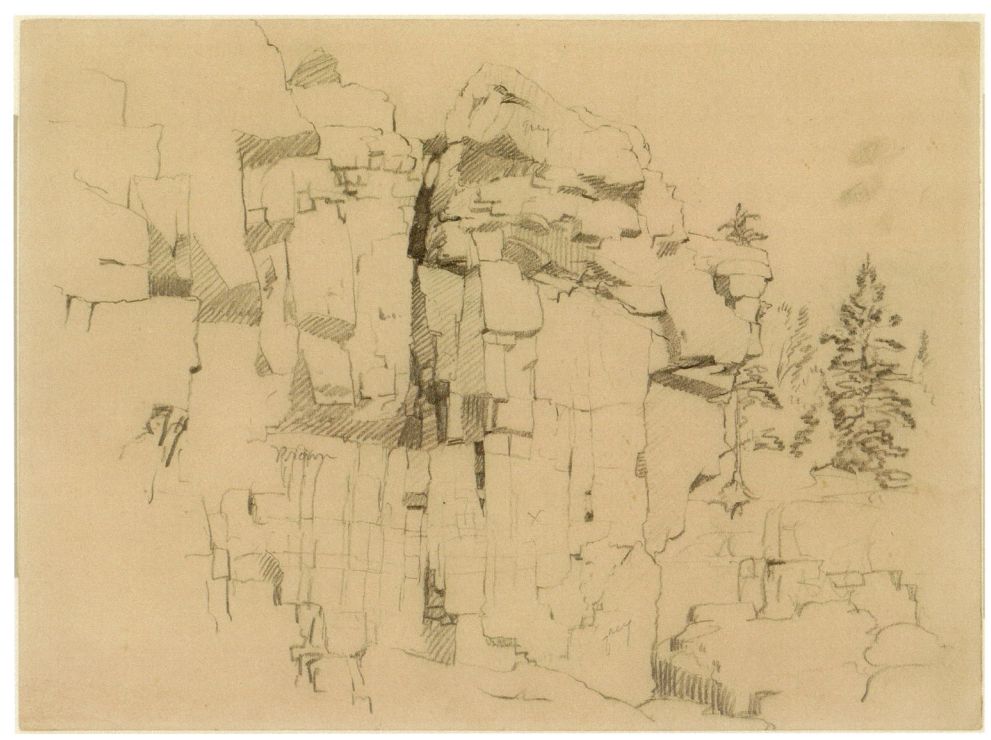

Fig. 9. Frederic Edwin Church, *Granite Cliffs, Mount Desert Island*, c. August 1850, graphite on light brown paper, 10¹³⁄₁₆ × 15 in., OL.1977.112

Understandably, he was eager to visit particular views his mentor Cole had sketched earlier, a beautiful example being the double-page panorama he drew of the Porcupine Islands (*Sols Cliff and the Porcupine Islands*) (fig. 6). A small boat took him to the outer island in the Bay, Ironbound, noted for the sheer vertical cliffs on its south side (fig. 7). Here Church made a bold drawing, *Cliffs on One of the Porcupine Islands* (fig. 8), dividing his sheet vertically down the center with the cliff face in the foreground, intersected by the horizon line of the far shore. Other Cole views that Church reprised were Otter Cliffs (*Granite Cliffs, Mount Desert Island*) (fig. 9), a close-up sketch of the compressed cubic blocks of quartz and granite across the rock face (fig. 10), and *Sand Beach* (fig. 11). On the beach itself he primed a sheet of paperboard with a reddish-tan ground, on which he half finished an oil study of the rocky coast nearby. A companion oil study, also half completed, looked northward across Sand Beach to a pastoral farm expanse beneath Newport Mountain (fig. 12).

Church was fascinated with the glacial geology of Mount Desert, and his refined talents as a draftsman were perfectly suited to capturing the facets of rock formations and the light and shadow defining their structure (fig. 13). In a format similar to his drawing of the cliffs at Ironbound Island, he outlined the rising rock formation of *Stone Pillar, Mount Desert Island* (fig. 14) in juxtaposition to the distant horizon line. Shortly, he would make use of this play between foreground and background, vertical and horizontal, in

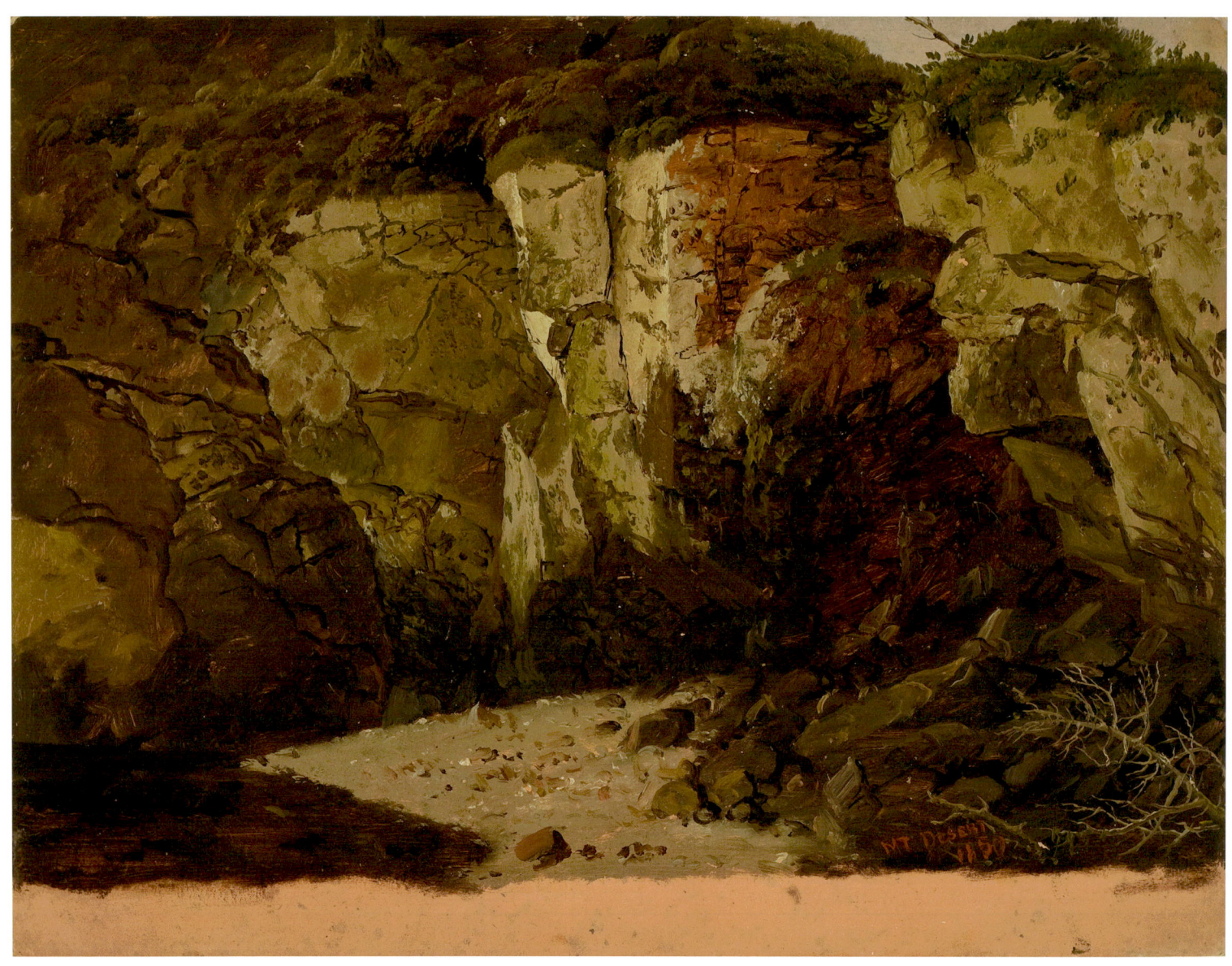

Fig. 10. Frederic Edwin Church, *Cliffs and Rocky Cove, Mount Desert Island*, c. August 1850, oil on light brown cardboard, 12⅛ × 16⅛ in., OL.1978.22

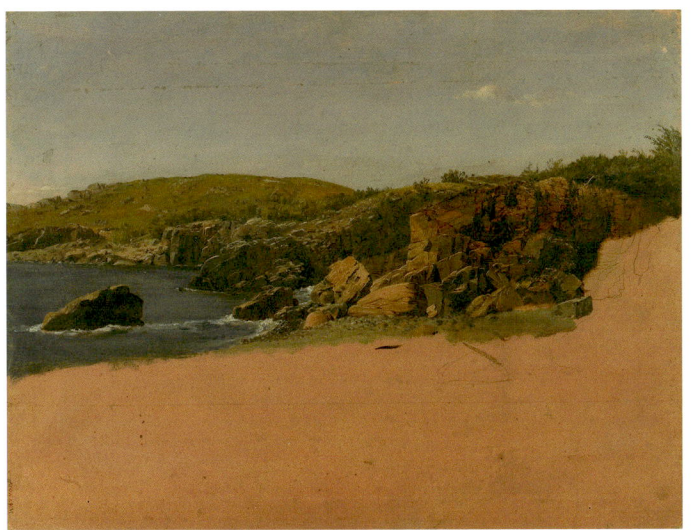

Fig. 11. Frederic Edwin Church, *Coast at Mount Desert (Sand Beach)*, c. 1850, oil and graphite on cardboard, 12 × 16¹⁄₁₆ in., Cooper-Hewitt National Design Museum, Smithsonian Institution, New York, Gift of Louis P. Church, 1917-4-645. Photograph: Matt Flynn, Image Courtesy Cooper-Hewitt National Design Museum/Art Resource, NY

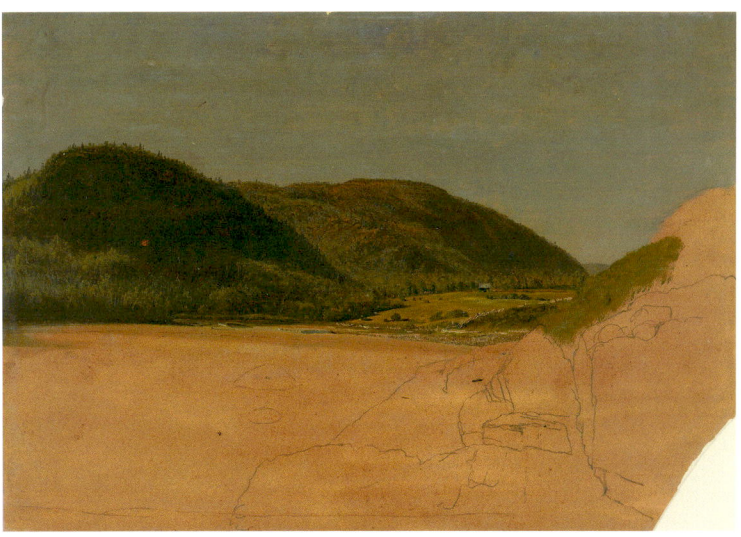

Fig. 12. Frederic Edwin Church, *The Beehive and Sand Beach from Great Head, Mount Desert*, c. 1850, oil and graphite on cardboard, 10½ × 15½ in., Cooper-Hewitt National Design Museum, Smithsonian Institution, New York, Gift of Louis P. Church, 1917-4-1368. Photograph: Matt Flynn, Image Courtesy Cooper-Hewitt National Design Museum/Art Resource, NY

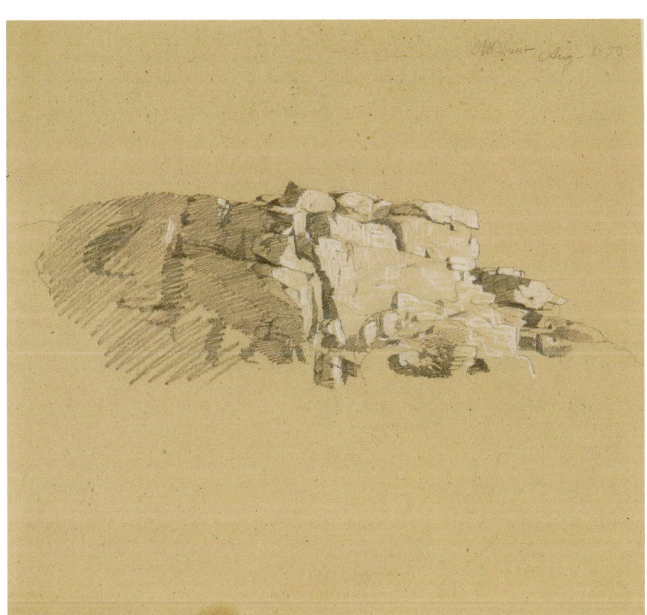

Fig. 13. Frederic Edwin Church, *Rock Outcropping, Mount Desert Island*, August 1850, graphite and gouache on coarse light brown paper, 11³⁄₁₆ × 12⅜ in., OL.1980.1445

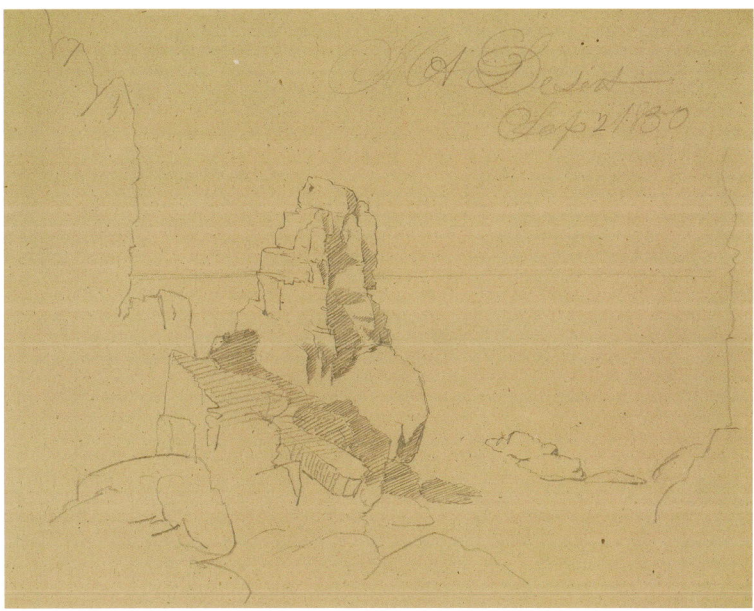

Fig. 14. Frederic Edwin Church, *Stone Pillar, Mount Desert Island*, September 2, 1850, graphite on coarse light brown paper, 11¼ × 14½ in., OL.1980.1450 recto

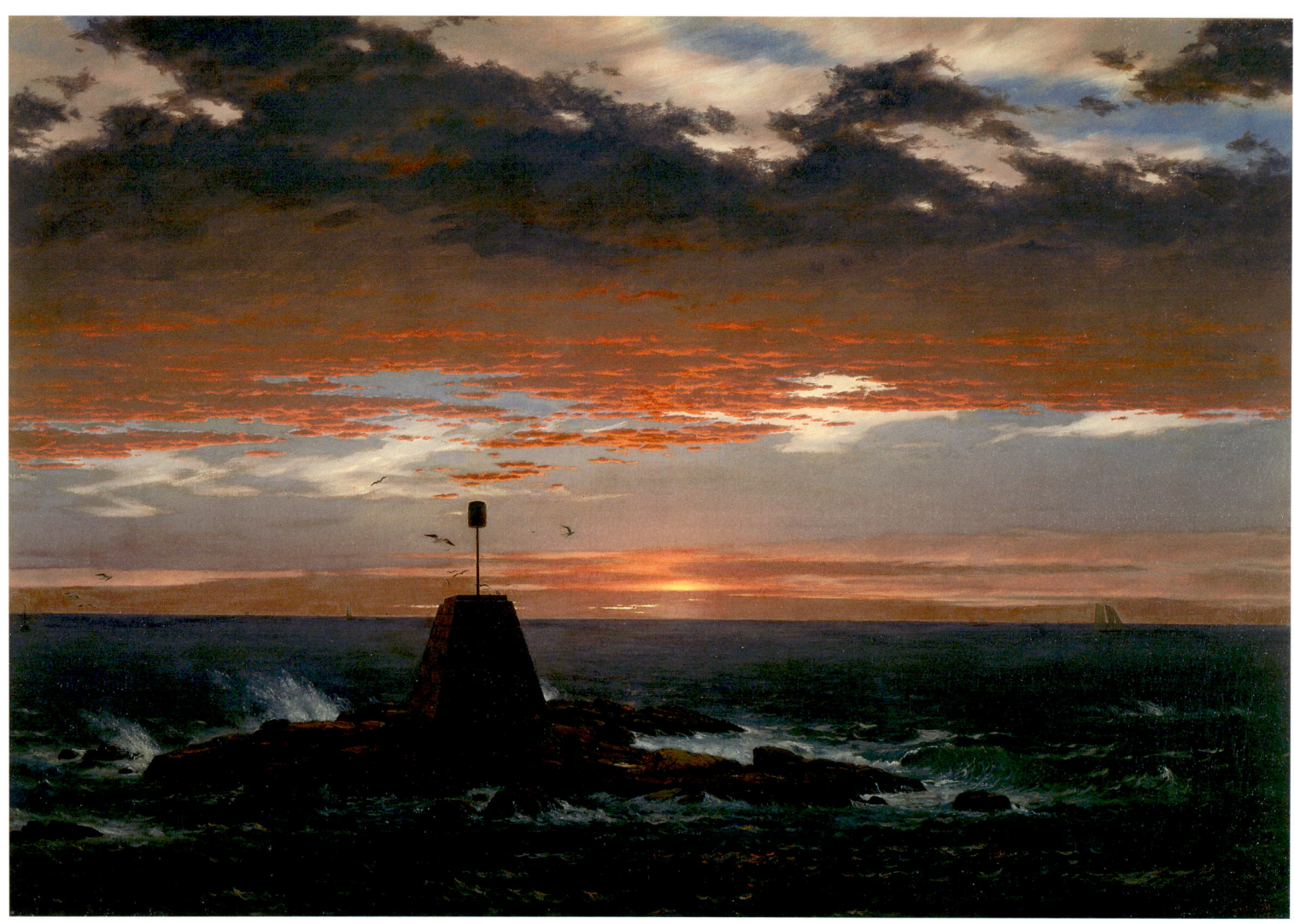

Fig. 15. Frederic Edwin Church, *Beacon, off Mount Desert Island*, 1851, oil on canvas, 31 × 46 in., Private Collection

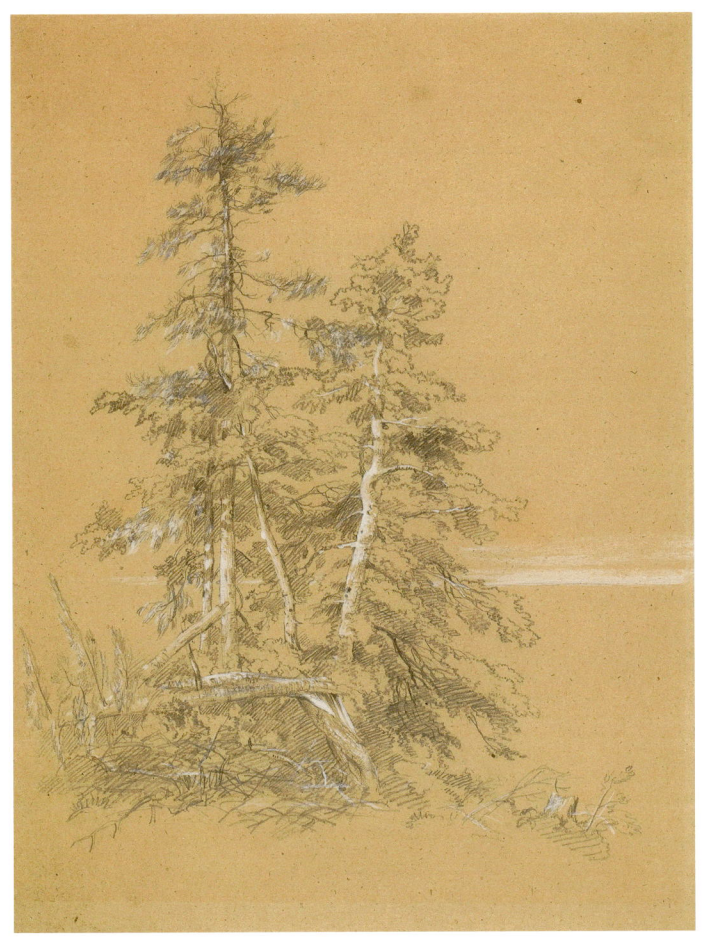

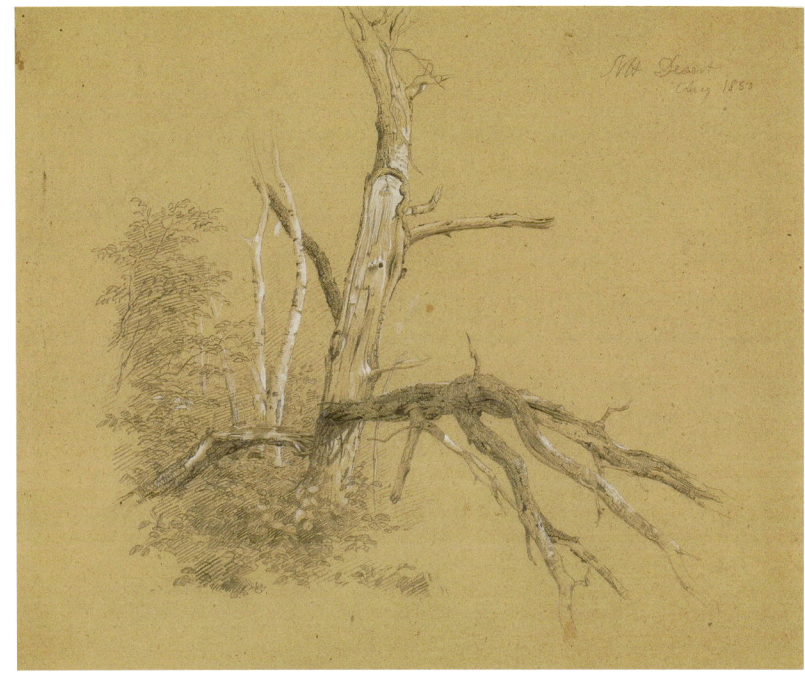

his first great Maine sunrise painting, *Beacon, off Mount Desert Island*, 1851 (fig. 15). Meanwhile, during those three summer months of 1850 he energetically sketched a broad variety of island scenes and landscape details. He made precise studies of *Evergreen Trees* (fig. 16), probably spruce, and of lightning-blasted tree trunks, *Birch Tree Trunk and Twisted Branches*, c. August 1850 (Olana State Historic Site) and *Birch Tree Struck by Lightning* (fig. 17). These were in the manner of Cole, suggesting God's hand in the life of nature, but were far more specific and identifiable in their execution.

While Cole's elements of nature were usually generalized and often metaphoric, referencing universal stages of growth and decay, Church regularly made explicit notations of times of day and tide, lighting conditions, and atmospheric effects. To this end he heightened his dark graphite lines on gray or neutral papers with passages of Chinese white chalk to indicate particular highlights on the water or cloud formations in the sky. A good example is *Prow of Rock, Porcupine Island* (fig. 18), which bears extensive notes like "very few white Barnacles . . . yellow and rusty light. . . . Flood tide just commenced . . .

Fig. 16. Frederic Edwin Church, *Evergreen Trees, Mount Desert Island*, c. August 1850, graphite and gouache on coarse light brown paper, 14⅝ × 11¼ in., OL.1980.1990

Fig. 17. Frederic Edwin Church, *Birch Tree Struck by Lightning, Mount Desert Island*, August 1850, graphite and gouache on coarse light brown paper, 11¹³⁄₁₆ × 14⁹⁄₁₆ in., OL.1980.1442

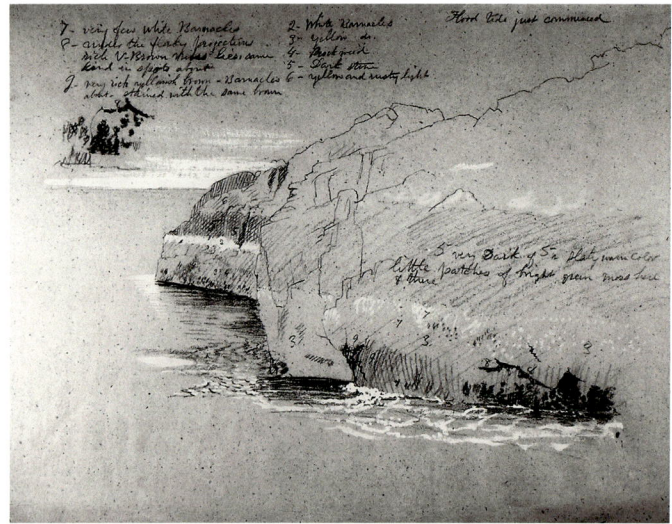

Fig. 18. Frederic Edwin Church, *Prow of Rock, Porcupine Island,* c. August 1850, graphite and gouache on coarse light brown paper, 11¼ × 14¾ in., OL.1977.52

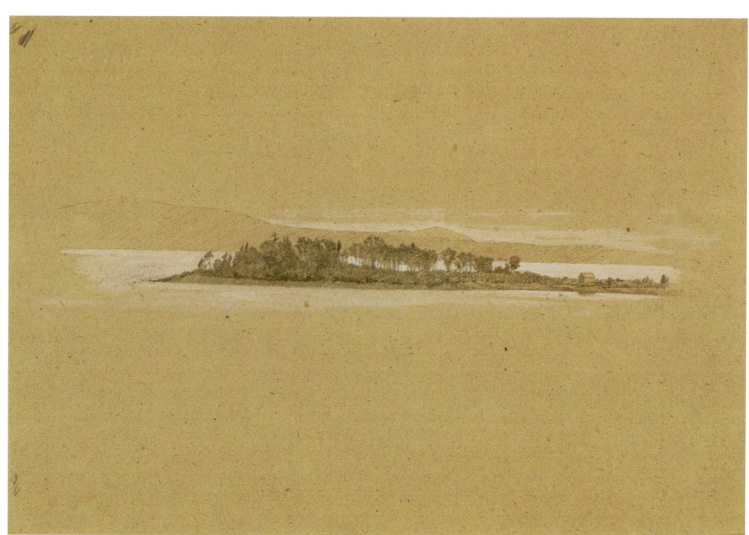

Fig. 19. Frederic Edwin Church, *Peninsula in Somes Sound, Mount Desert Island,* c. July – August 1850, graphite and gouache on coarse brown paper, 7⅝ × 11¼ in., OL.1980.1507

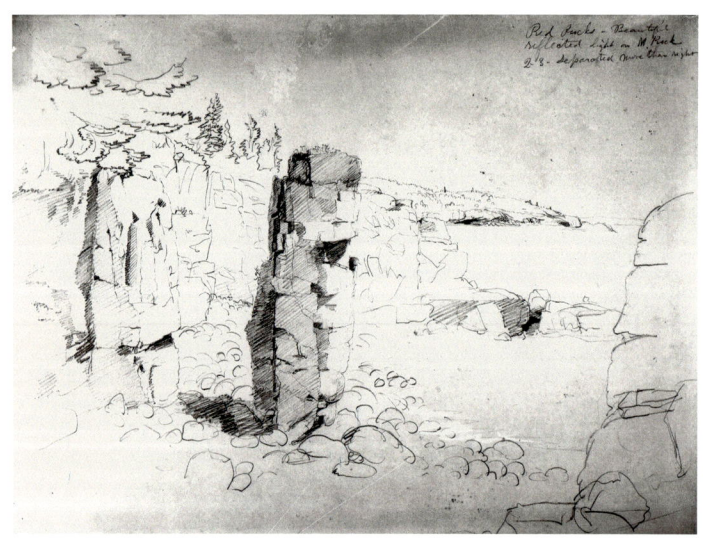

Fig. 20. Frederic Edwin Church, *Monument Rock, Mount Desert Island,* c. August 1850, graphite and gouache on light brown paper, 11⅝ × 15⅝ in., OL.1977.116 verso

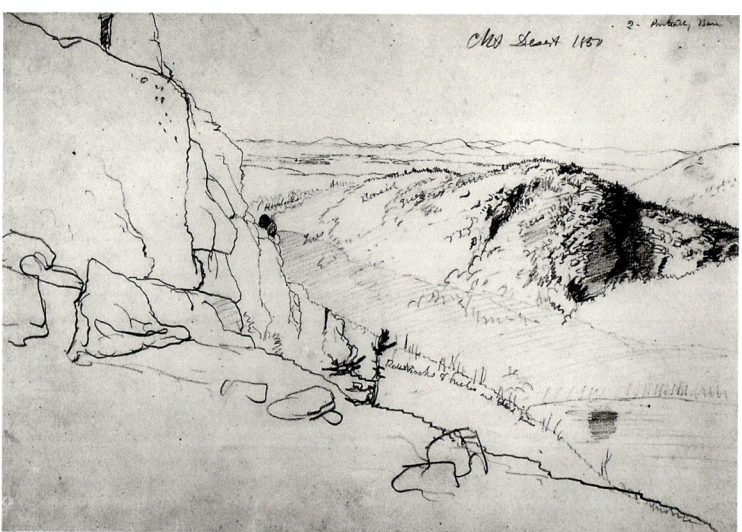

Fig. 21. Frederic Edwin Church, *Mount Desert Island from Dorr Mountain,* c. July – August 1850, graphite on buff paper, 9⅞ × 14⅞ in., OL.1980.1454 recto

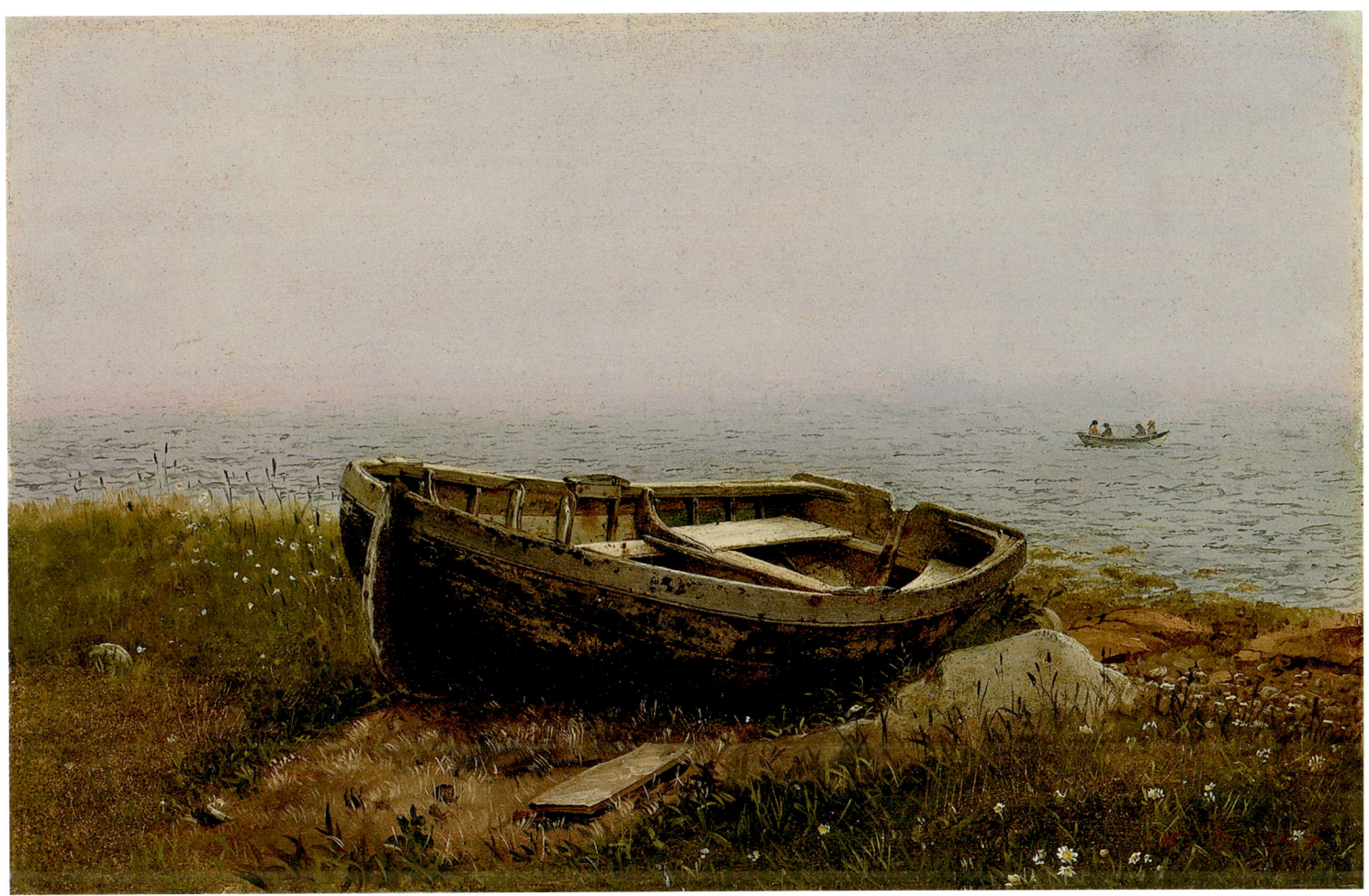

little patches of bright green moss here & there."[9] Strokes of Chinese white are especially effective in the simple but striking drawing titled *Peninsula in Somes Sound* (fig. 19), with its band of light over the distant hills and sun glare across the water. Church hiked long stretches of the coastline, recording unusual rock piles (*Monument Rock*) (fig. 20) and inland vistas from the mountain ridges and summits, high enough to get broad glimpses of the waters surrounding the island, for instance, *View from Jordan Ridge, Mount Desert Island*, July 1850 (Olana State Historic Site) and *Mount Desert Island from Dorr Mountain* (fig. 21) (more likely also from Jordan Mountain).[10]

Several important oil paintings resulted from these summer sketches, some smaller ones dated 1850 executed on the spot, and several larger canvases completed over the next year back in New York and intended for exhibition at the National Academy. One charming shoreline scene (*The Old Boat*) *Abandoned Skiff*, 1851 (fig. 22), depicted the hull of an old rowboat pulled up from the water's edge and resting among tall grasses and

Fig. 22. Frederic Edwin Church (*The Old Boat*), *Abandoned Skiff*, 1851, oil on cardboard, 11 × 17 in., Museo Thyssen-Bornemisza, Madrid, 509 (1982.40). Image © Museo Thyssen-Bornemisza, Madrid

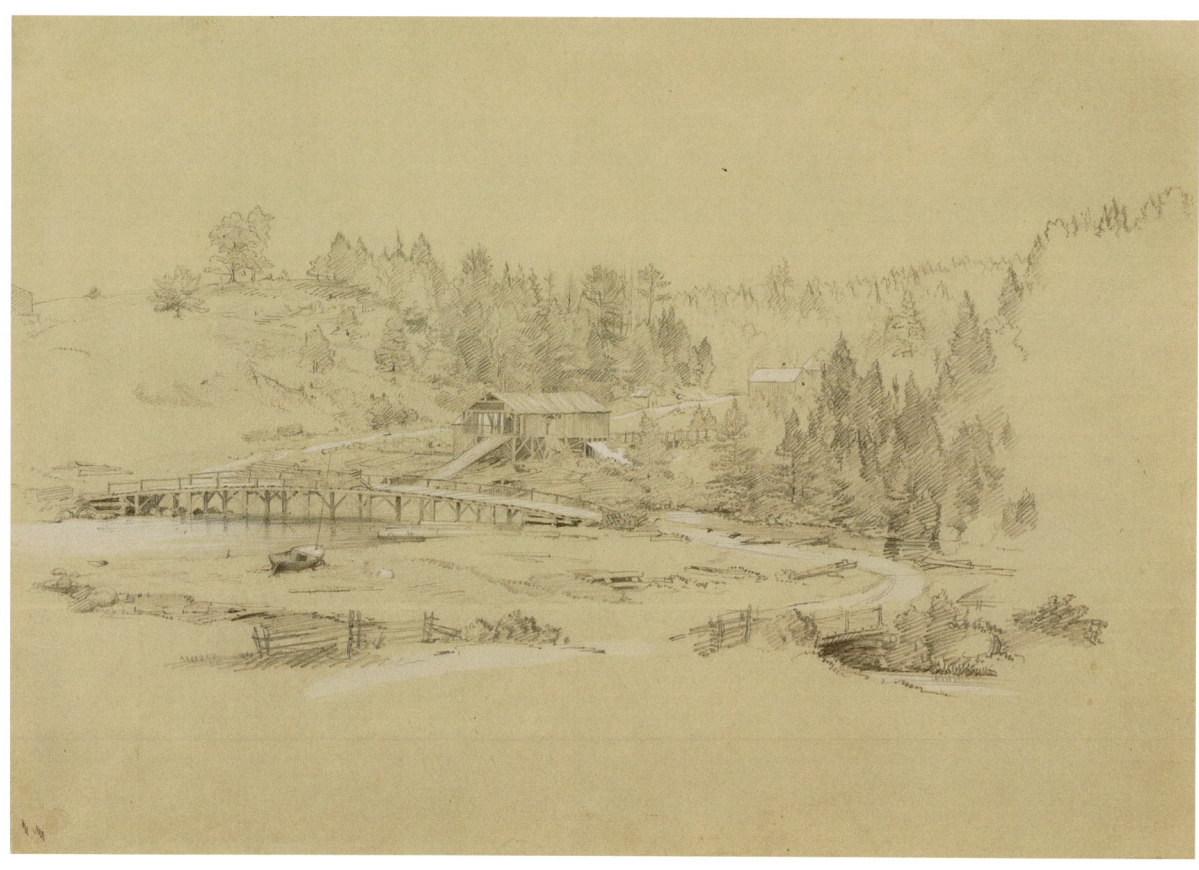

Fig. 23. Frederic Edwin Church, *Lumber Mill, Mount Desert Island*, c. July–August 1850, graphite, gouache, and chalk on gray-green paper, 10¼ × 15 in., OL.1980.1610

wild daisies. Offshore a few figures are rowing in, with the glare of fog pressing behind. Fog was a frequent summer phenomenon and sometimes frustrated the artist, but he also loved to record its white vaporous effects. Observing the incoming bank here, Church noted, "We have just got into the edge of one, which, however, has not prevented our transferring to canvas an old hull of a boat and some rocks this morning."[11]

Lumber mills were under construction and in operation at various locations around the island at this time, providing a growing business up and down the coast. Church, followed by William Stanley Haseltine a few years later, found them a lively subject to sketch, as seen in *Lumber Mill, Sullivan, Maine*, 1850 (Olana State Historic Site), and *Lumber Mill, Mount Desert Island* (fig. 23), of probably the same date, the latter providing the basis for a beautifully finished oil (fig. 24). The preparatory drawing is unusually densely worked, with precise rendering of the mill building, nearby wood bridges, and related domestic structures tucked into the woods behind. The completed painting possesses a suffusing pastoral tranquillity, created by the surrounding forest greenery, soft yellow light falling on the open fields, and billowing fair weather clouds rising behind the hillside.

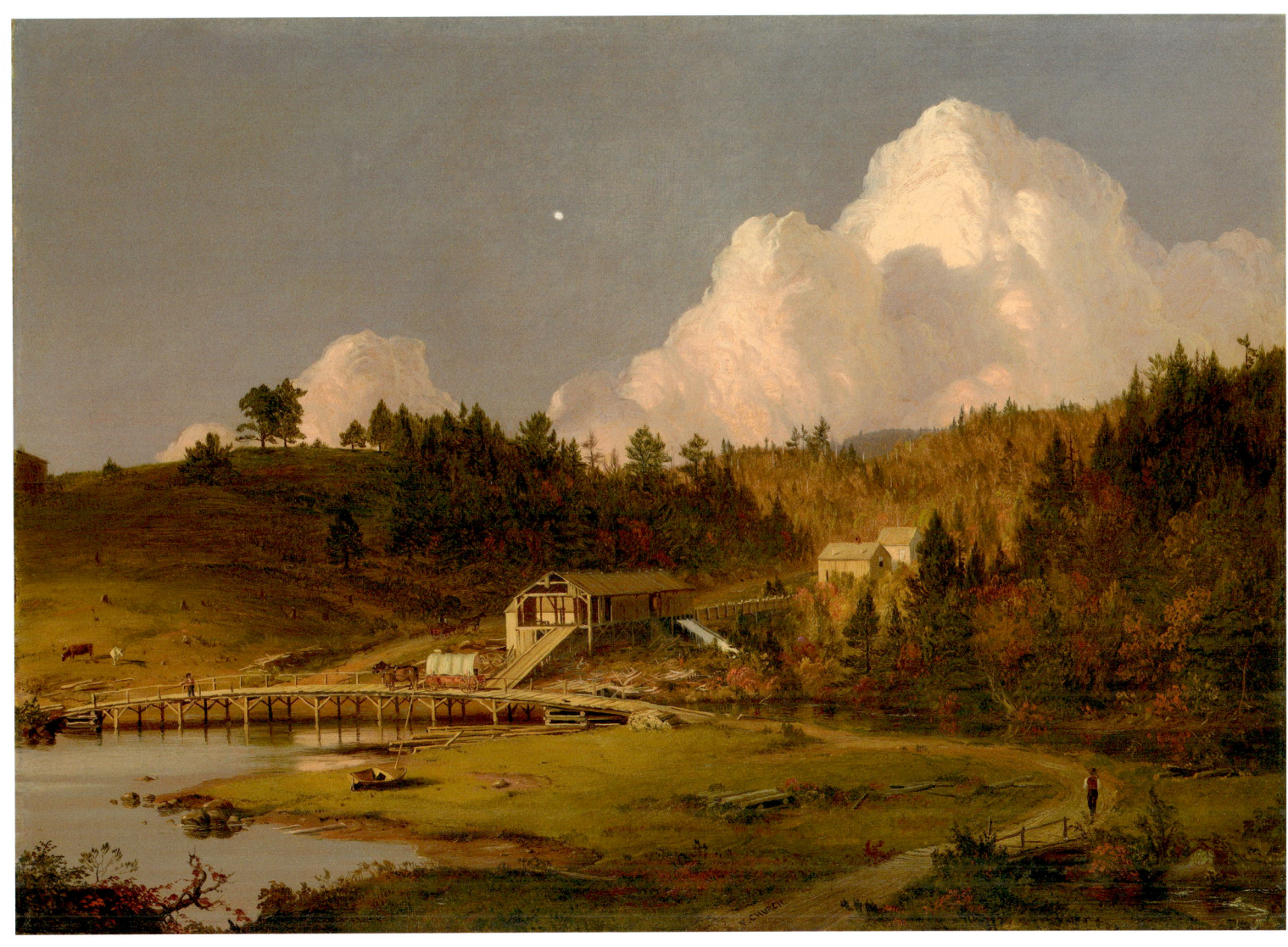

Fig. 24. Frederic Edwin Church, *Lumber Mill,
Mount Desert*, c. 1850, oil on canvas, 14 × 20 in.,
Private Collection. Image Courtesy David
Stansbury

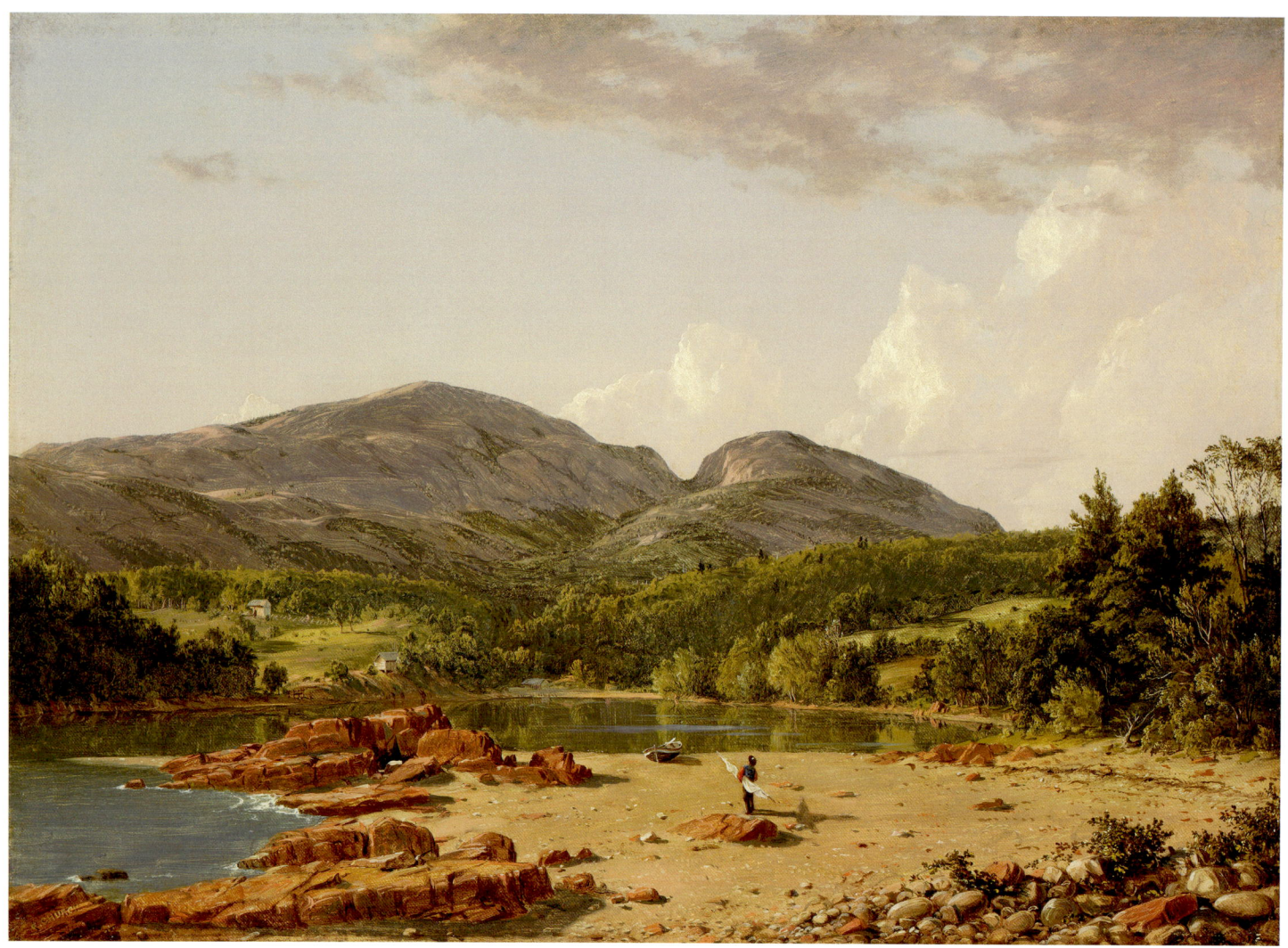

Fig. 25. Frederic Edwin Church, *Otter Creek, Mt. Desert*, 1850, oil on canvas, 16¾ × 24 in., Museum of Fine Arts Boston, Seth K. Sweetser Fund, Tompkins Collection—Arthur Gordon Tompkins Fund, Henry H. and Zoe Oliver Sherman Fund and Gift of Mrs. R. Amory Thorndike, 1982.419. Image © 2012 Museum of Fine Arts, Boston

By contrast, Church gave a more monumental treatment in the sublime mode to his larger canvases of Newport and Green Mountains. *Otter Creek, Mt. Desert*, 1850 (fig. 25), looks toward Green and Dry Mountains (now Cadillac and Dorr) with the dip of its gorge between them. They rise impressively before the small figure gazing up in the foreground, a grounded sailing skiff beyond, and across the creek a prospering farmstead in the background. This formula of fusing dramatic and tranquil elements in the same picture would take on new intensity in canvases of the next few years. Historians have pointed out that the furled sail held by the standing figure casts a shadow on the adjacent ground in the form of a cross, suggesting a spiritual inflection to this landscape experience.

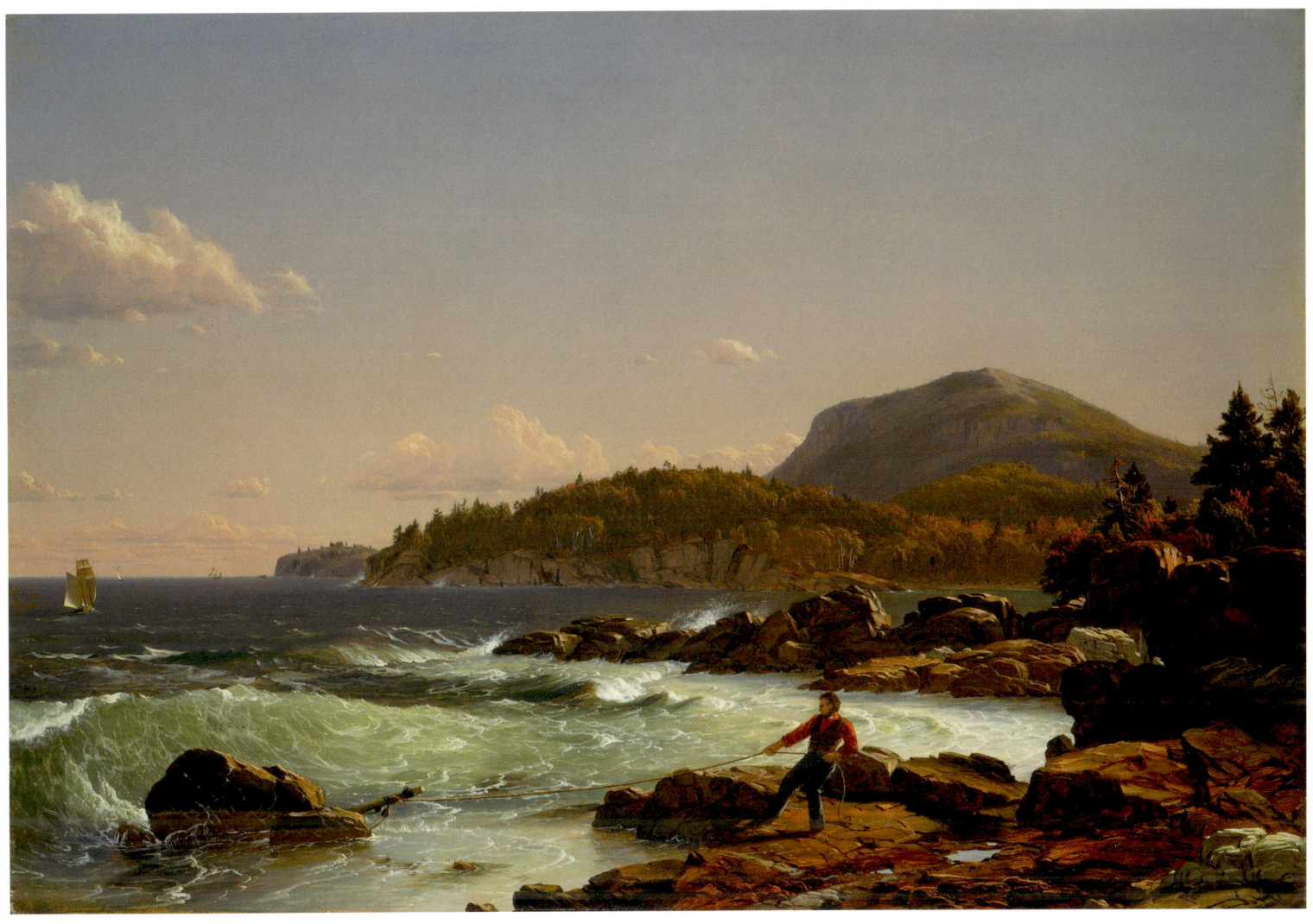

Just to the east Church undertook several drawings of Newport Mountain from varying distances away and slightly different angles, almost as if he were photographing with changing zoom and wide-angle lenses. When he got back to his New York studio in the fall, he began to compose a large canvas of the view (fig. 26), synthesizing selected aspects he had recorded by pencil on separate sheets. This painting also features a man in the foreground, giving scale, here pulling in over the rocks the remains of a wrecked vessel. While the sky is a crisp deep blue and autumn colors dot the forests, it is the turbulent surf and looming mountainside that address nature's more awesome character.

Fig. 26. Frederic Edwin Church, *Newport Mountain, Mount Desert*, 1851, oil on canvas, 21¼ × 31¼ in., Private Collection, promised gift, National Gallery of Art, Washington, D.C.

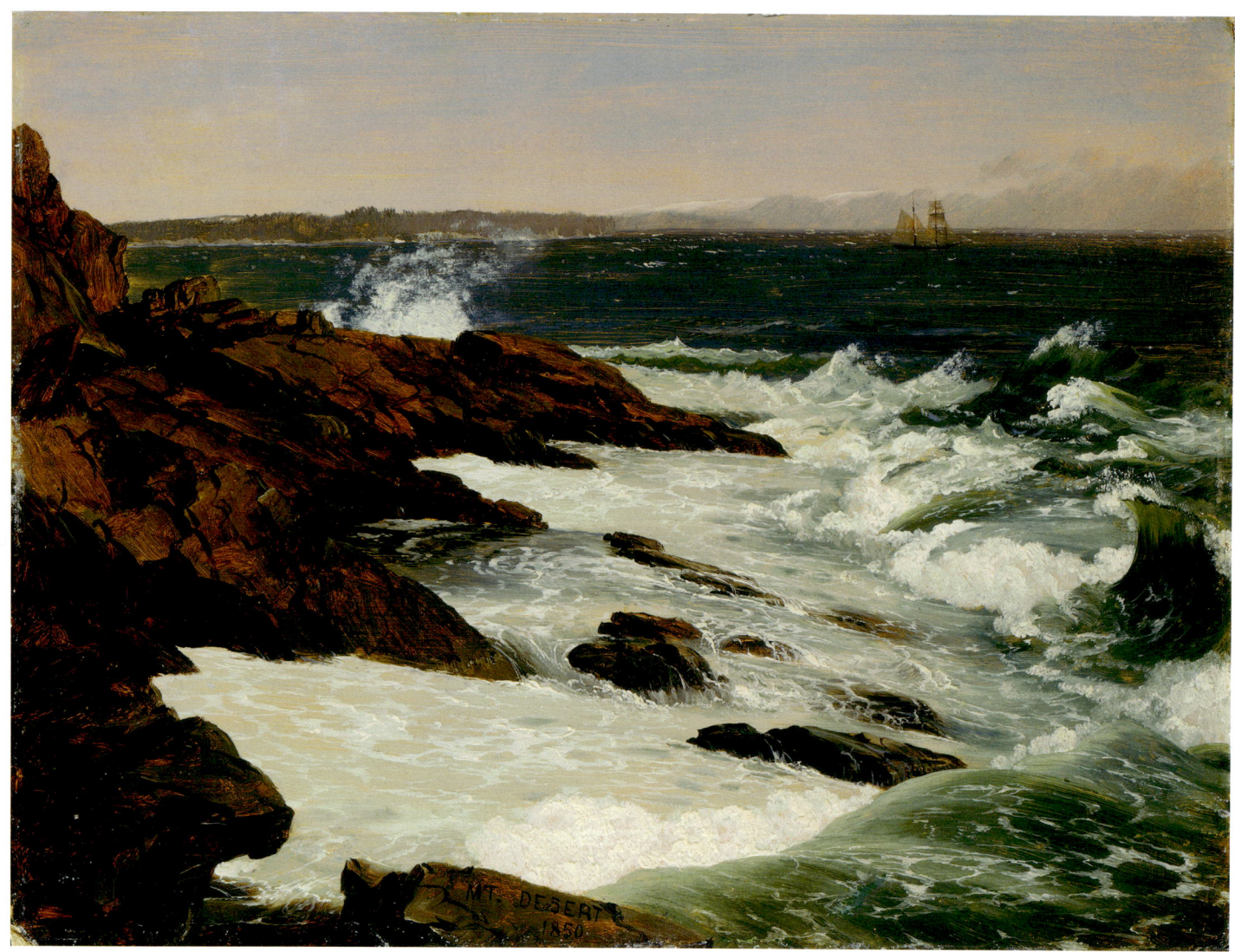

Fig. 27. Frederic Edwin Church, *Fog off Mount Desert*, 1850, oil on academy board, 11½ × 15½ in., Private Collection, promised gift, National Gallery of Art, Washington, D.C.

Though Church regularly annotated his drawings with observations about light and color, as we have seen, he also periodically made outdoor oil studies on paperboard, and at least two of these dated 1850, *Rough Surf* (Private Collection) and *Fog off Mount Desert* (fig. 27), are small miracles of meticulous technical execution. He employed his familiar red ground primer, particularly expressive in conveying the sense of the surf thinning out as it washes up over the sand and pink granite ledges. Unlike Cole, who had tended to paint all the components of his landscapes with similar brushwork, Church adjusted his applications of paint to the specific textures of different natural elements. So it is foamy in breaking waves, thinner for water sliding over rocks, broad and solid for the dark granite, and wispy for the fog bank forming over Schoodic Point on the other side of Frenchman's Bay. In these finished studies we almost feel the physics of water's action, even as certain passages take on near abstract qualities in their rhythmic patterning.

Perhaps the masterpiece of this early group of paintings was *Beacon, off Mount Desert Island* (see fig. 15), the result of several unrelated preliminary sketches. We are looking over the pyramidal stone day marker at East Bunker's Ledge, which marks the entrance of the so-called Eastern Way into the great harbor of Mount Desert. It was one of the early markers placed by the government along the East Coast in the early nineteenth century, and Church would have seen it on his first passage into Seal Harbor. He sketched it on a sheet with other random renderings of local schooners (fig. 28), one half shrouded in fog passing the shore. On another page marked "Aug 19—Monday morning" he drew the horizon line high across the paper (fig. 29), dotted with the staccato of endless fishing vessel sails we might calculate as several dozen, which he wrote were "about one half the actual number seen."

After the summer he also had in his portfolio another small oil study of *Schoodic Peninsula from Mount Desert at Sunrise* (fig. 30), striking for its massive red-tinged cloud

Fig. 28. Frederic Edwin Church, *Study of Schooners and Beacon Day Marker*, c. 1850, graphite and gouache on olive green wove paper, 9⅞ × 7³⁄₁₆ in., Cooper-Hewitt National Design Museum, Smithsonian Institution, New York, Gift of Louis P. Church, 1917-4-271-a. Photograph: Matt Flynn, Image Courtesy Cooper-Hewitt National Design Museum / Art Resource, NY

Fig. 29. Frederic Edwin Church, *Fleet of Mackerel Fishers*, August 1850, graphite on off-white wove paper, 8⁷⁄₁₆ × 13¹¹⁄₁₆ in., Cooper-Hewitt National Design Museum, Smithsonian Institution, New York, Gift of Louis P. Church, 1917-4-7. Photograph: Matt Flynn, Image Courtesy Cooper-Hewitt National Design Museum/Art Resource, NY

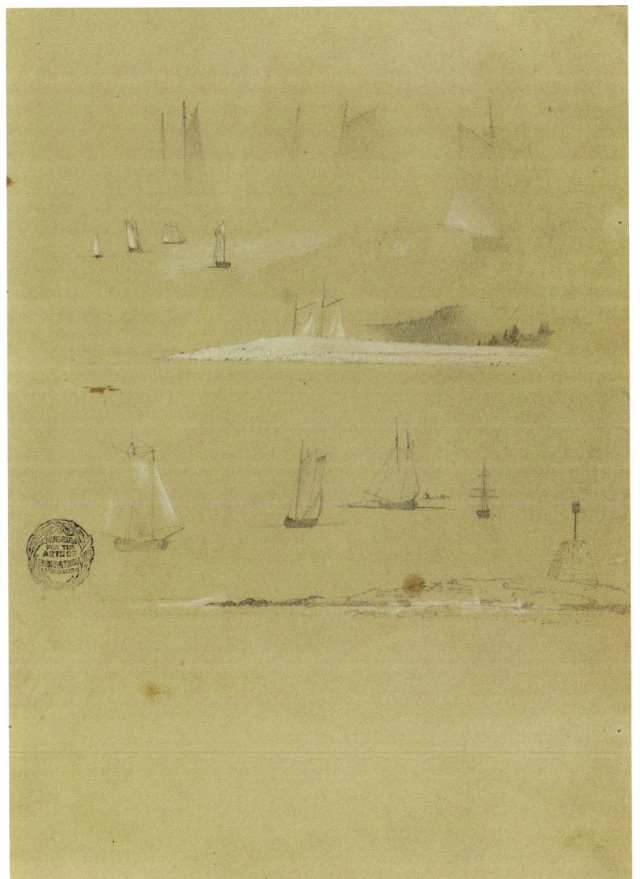

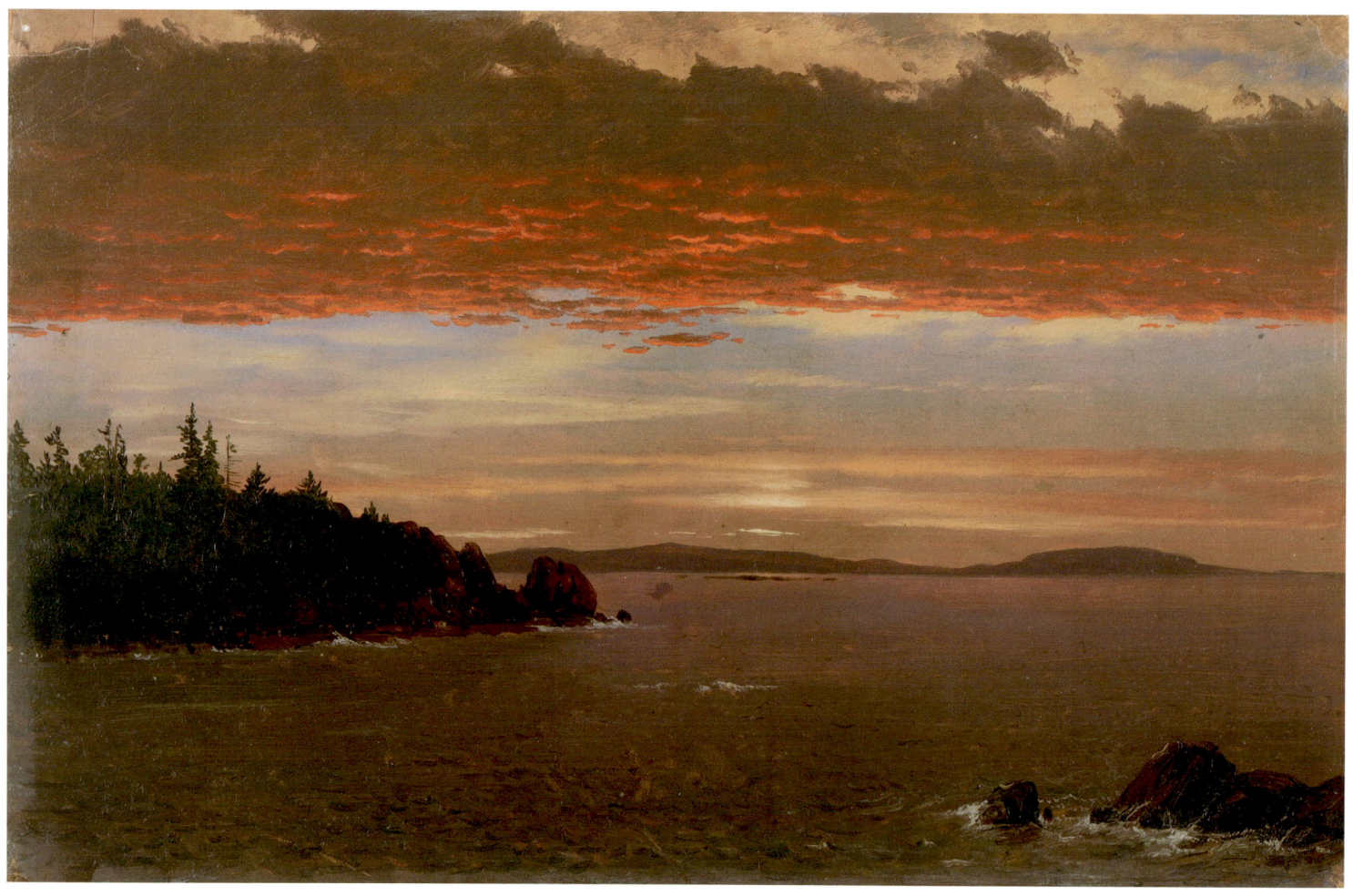

Fig. 30. Frederic Edwin Church, *Schoodic Peninsula from Mount Desert at Sunrise*, 1850–55, oil on paperboard, 8⁵⁄₁₆ × 14 in., Cooper-Hewitt National Design Museum, Smithsonian Institution, New York, Gift of Louis P. Church, 1917-4-332. Photograph: Matt Flynn, Image Courtesy Cooper-Hewitt National Design Museum/Art Resource, NY

band across the upper sky. We can only imagine his delight in pulling these sketches together to compose the final oil. The mackerel fleet is gone, save one schooner on the horizon, the cloud bank nearly doubled in depth, and the day marker prominent in the foreground. Although the scene is demonstrably based on observing the first rays of sun in the east, some have further attributed spiritual connotations to the image, alluding to the Christian sense of resurrection in day's beginning and hopeful promise.

Sunrise was also one of Thoreau's favorite times of day, and he celebrated dawn in his journals as well as his first book, *A Week on the Concord and Merrimack Rivers*, published in 1849. As with Church, this moment of day's creation was both a physical and spiritual experience. His second day on the river Thoreau observed, "It was a quiet Sunday morning, with more of the auroral rosy and white than of the yellow light in it, as if it dated from earlier than the fall of man. . . ." And the following morning he talked of "when the first light dawned on the earth, and the birds awoke, and the brave river was heard rippling confidently seaward, and the nimble early rising wind rustled the oak leaves. . . ."[12] Church thought highly enough of his first sunrise painting as well as of the Newport Mountain canvas and the two small surf paintings to send them to the Art Union for exhibition that year. It was one of his most productive periods of work, during which he absorbed and transcended his multiple sources of inspiration.

He returned to Mount Desert in October 1851 and again actively painted there, while also venturing further east to the large island of Grand Manan on the Canadian border. These experiences led to two significant canvases, *Grand Manan Island, Bay of Fundy* (fig. 31) and *The Wreck* (see fig. 4), both finished in 1852 and exploiting the radiating coloration of his cadmium pigments. As in previous canvases, the first included a red-shirted figure walking in the foreground, one of Church's last compositional debts to

Fig. 31. Frederic Edwin Church, *Grand Manan Island, Bay of Fundy,* 1852, oil on canvas, 21¹³⁄₁₆ × 31⁵⁄₁₆ in., Wadsworth Atheneum Museum of Art, Hartford, Gallery Fund, 1898.6

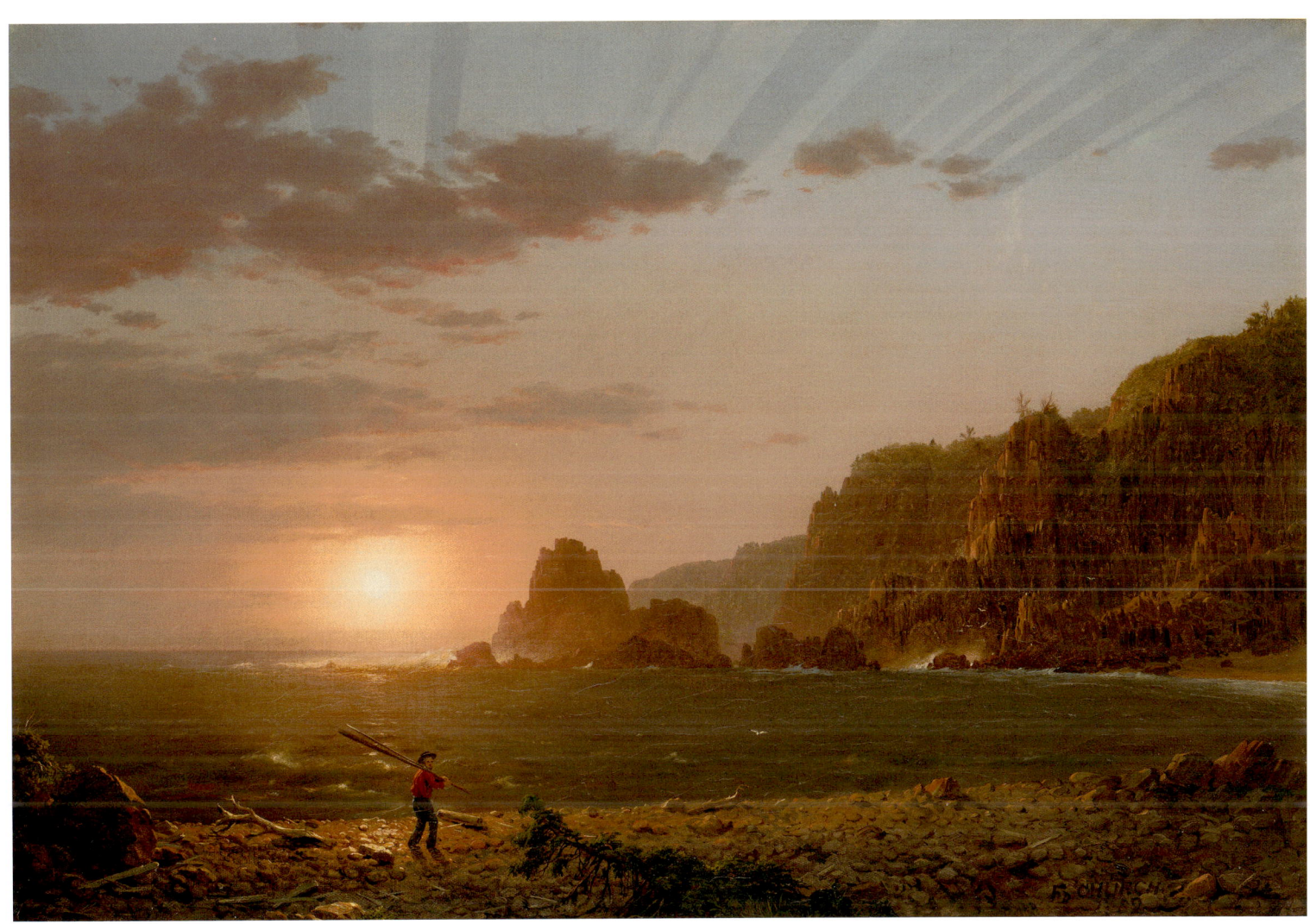

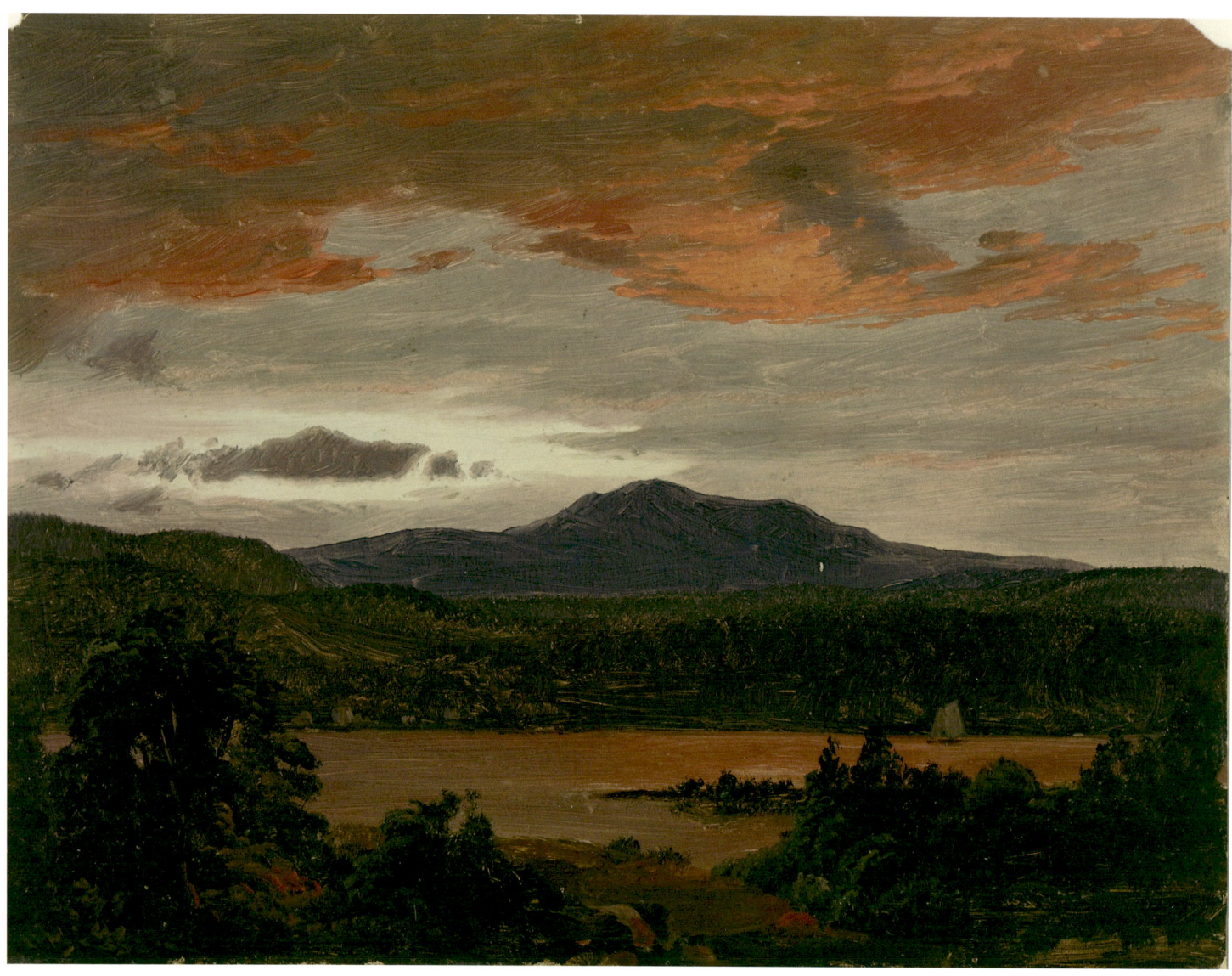

Fig. 32. Frederic Edwin Church, *Mount Katahdin from Lake Katahdin, Maine*, c. 1852, oil on thin paperboard, 8¹⁵⁄₁₆ × 11¹⁵⁄₁₆ in., Cooper-Hewitt National Design Museum, Smithsonian Institution, New York, Gift of Louis P. Church, 1917-4-323c. Photograph: Matt Flynn, Image Courtesy Cooper-Hewitt National Design Museum/Art Resource, NY

Cole and Lane. This was also an early morning scene, with the glowing sun tingeing the island's towering cliff walls. However, in the second picture Church made some crucial changes: no human figures are present, and an old schooner forced onto the rocks now occupies the foreground. Its aft mast is broken, but the one forward with its cross bar above forms a clearly silhouetted cross against the sky in an image of salvation.[13] Brilliant afternoon sunlight breaks through the stormy clouds to illuminate the horizon line with its redemptive force. With this work Church decisively turned his attention to the evening hours, whose expressive colors he would explore in shifting ways over the rest of the decade.

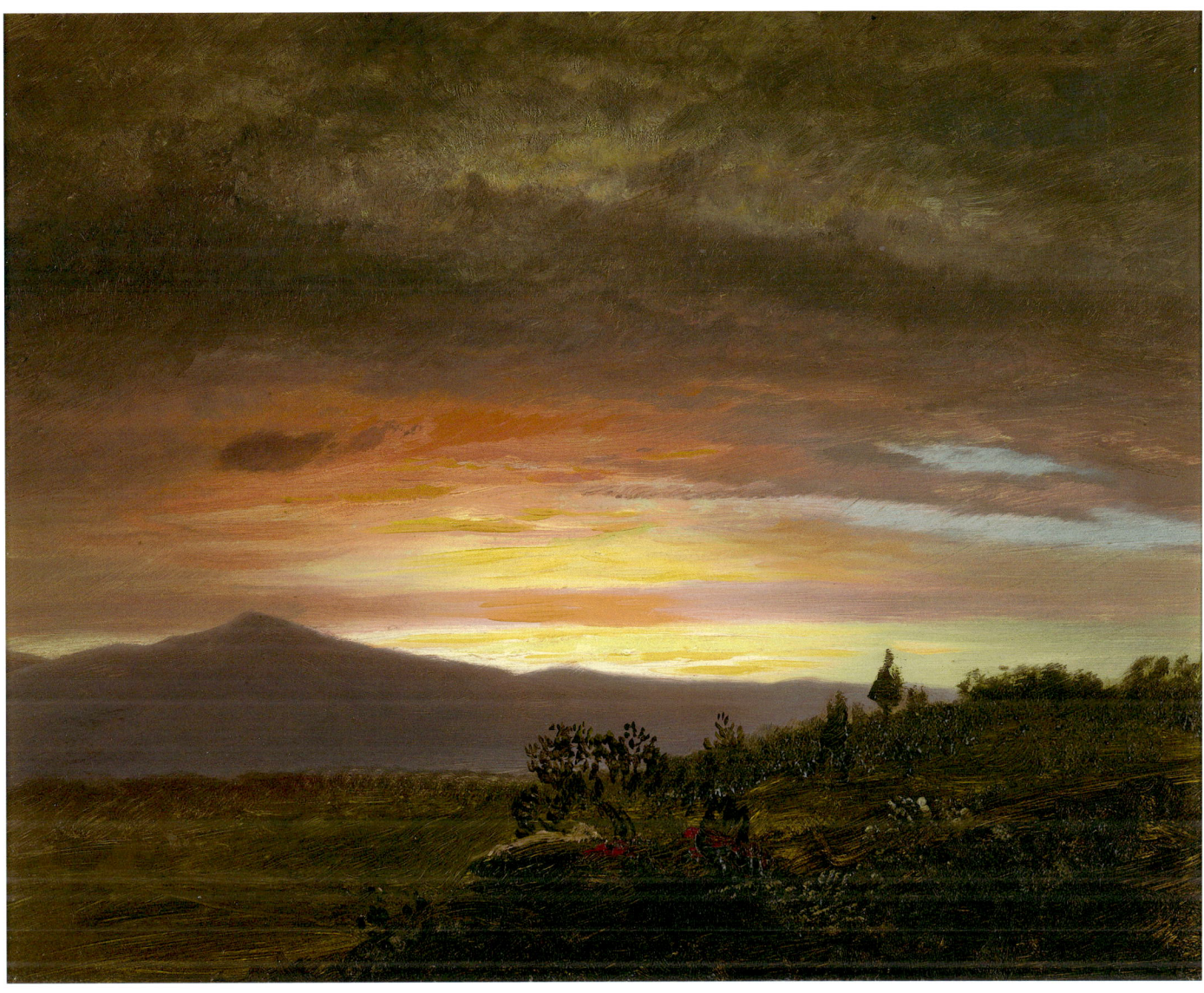

Also in 1852 Church made his first excursion to Mount Katahdin. Far fewer sketches survive from this trip, but the great northern peak clearly possessed his attention. Two powerful small oil studies depict the mountain silhouetted at twilight, *Mount Katahdin from Lake Katahdin* (fig. 32) and *Twilight, Mount Ktaadn* (fig. 33). Set in north central Maine in what is now Baxter State Park, and one of the highest in New England along with Mount Washington, Katahdin is also the result of combined volcanic and glacial activity. Because there are few competing foothills, it appears to rise dramatically in isolation from the surrounding landscape plain. It actually consists of two peaks, Pomola and Baxter (one its original Indian name, the other in honor of the land's donor

Fig. 33. Frederic Edwin Church, *Twilight, Mount Ktaadn*, c. 1858–60, oil on paper mounted on board, 10½ × 13⅝ in., Henry and Sharon Martin Collection

to the state), joined by a psychologically terrifying mile-long ridge known as the Knife Edge for its prevailing narrowness at the summit.

While he was revising drafts of *Walden* late in the summer of 1846, Thoreau said he spent "a fortnight in the woods of Maine," quite possibly prodded by an account of a trip to the mountain the year before by Edward Everett Hale and William Francis Channing that appeared in the *Boston Daily Advertiser*.[14] Thoreau traveled relatively easily from Boston to Bangor, then the lumbering capital of Maine, in a day, and made his way up the west branch of the Penobscot River to the mountain region. He sent the first section of his essay to Horace Greeley in New York for publication. It appeared in the July 1848 issue of John Sartain's *Union Magazine of Literature and Art*, with extracts also appearing the next year in the *Tribune* and *The Student*.

Thoreau's descriptions must have resonated in Church's mind as he approached and considered his own pictorial interpretation. The artist soon envisioned Katahdin as a sublime continental complement to the coastal positioning of Mount Desert. From his own trip came another great masterpiece executed in cadmium pigments, *Mount Ktaadn*, 1853 (fig. 34). It is really two separate pictures fused into one. Below is a pastoral vista not unlike the farm scenes he had just completed at Mount Desert. A dirt road crosses the stone bridge, domestic buildings and possibly a lumber mill nestle near the waterfall, cows idle in the shadows of a lake, and under a tree at the left a youth sits looking out toward the mountain peak. Almost none of this actually existed in Thoreau's or Church's day. Only impenetrable forests and Indian trails crossed this wilderness region. But for the artist this scene was symbolic of civilization's domestic settlement. Moreover, the boy's contemplation of the distance was pure Emersonian transcendentalism, where facing the western horizon meant looking to America's future, for it not only revealed God's presence in nature but forecast the nation's continental expansion.

On a follow-up trip Thoreau mentioned the "immeasurable forest for the sun to shine on. . . . No clearing, no house. It did not look as if a solitary traveler had cut so much as a walking-stick there. . . . Perhaps I most fully realized that this was primeval, untamed and forever untameable *Nature*."[15] This is what we see in the upper two-thirds of Church's composition, an awesome vision of nature's evening pyrotechnics extending over the bold lavender peak. Here is pure American wildness, in contrast to the settled terrain below. The painter has constructed a classic balance of the beautiful and the sublime, the civilized and the wild, held, as the country believed for a time at midcentury, in equilibrium. Such beliefs were made manifest in both ideas of distance and the meteorology of twilight.

Emerson set the theme when he said, "The health of the eye seems to demand a horizon. We are never tired, so long as we can see far enough."[16] Thoreau reflected further in his Journal for 1851: "The prospect of a vast horizon must be accessible in our

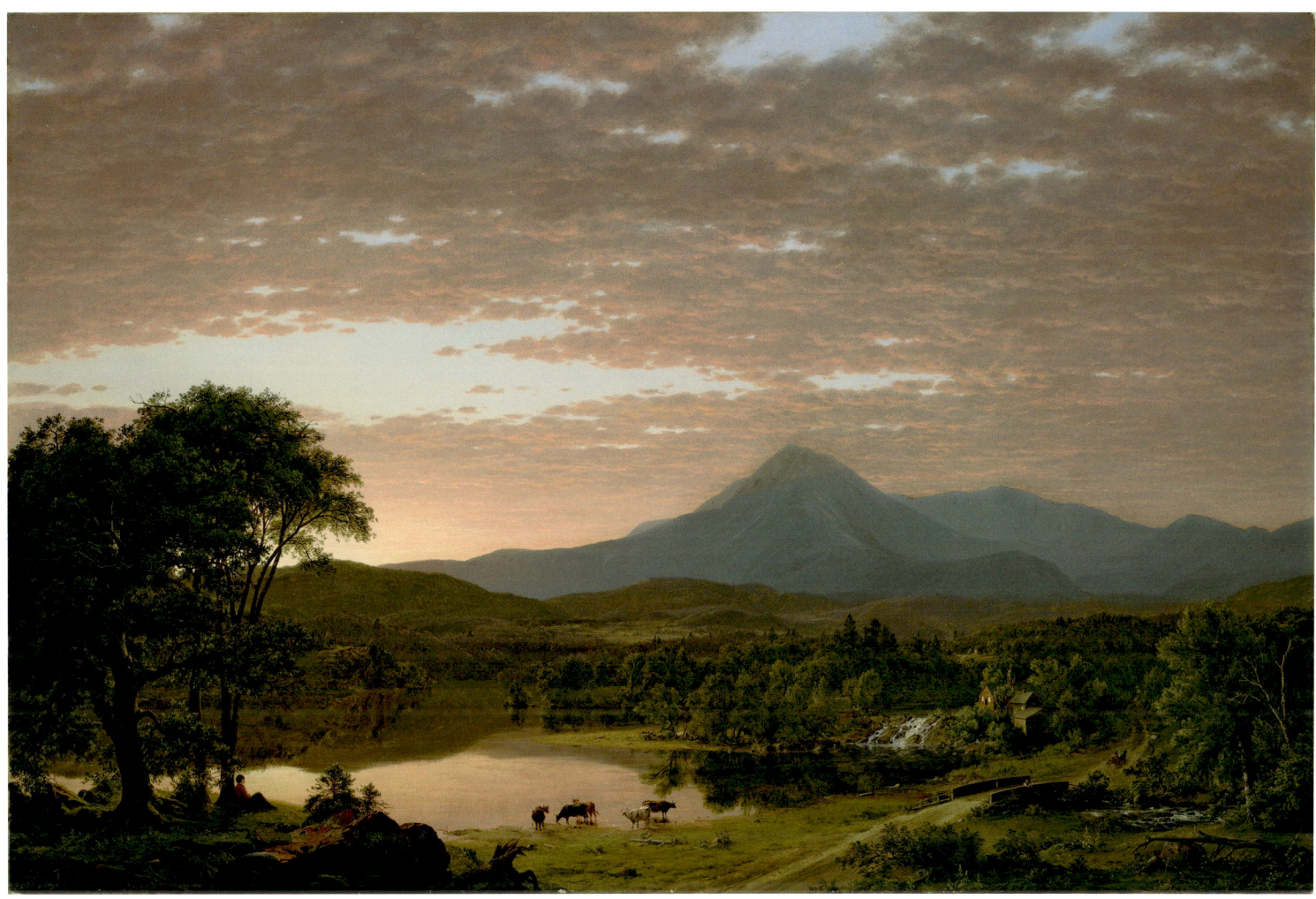

neighborhood. Where men of enlarged views may be educated." And later he asserted, "It is worth the while to see the *Mts* in the horizon once a day. . . . I wish to see the earth through the medium of much air or heaven—for there is no paint like the air. *Mts* thus seen are worthy of worship."[17]

At the same time Thoreau repeatedly wrote about sunset. It was both an optical and metaphorical occurrence: "Westward is Heaven or rather heavenward is the west. The way to heaven is from east to west around the earth. . . . The sun leads & shows it." "All the west horizon was glowing with a rosy border . . . as if the fires of the day had just been put out in the west and the burnt territory was sending out volumes of dun & lurid smoke to heaven." "The man is blessed who every day is permitted to behold anything so pure & serene as the western sky at sunset—while revolutions vex the world."[18] Church's Katahdin image embraces many of the same feelings: its sky is heroic

Fig. 34. Frederic Edwin Church, *Mount Ktaadn*, 1853, oil on canvas, 36¼ × 55¼ in., Yale University Art Gallery, New Haven, Stanley B. Resor, B.A. 1901, Fund, 1969.71

and inspirational, yet also reassuring and serene. Now the evening hour was both a sign of day's resolution and the promise of time's continuing cycle. Together, the two pieces of landscape make the scene at once local and continental, belonging to the present and the future.

Both Church and Thoreau at this moment sought to depict nature's polarities. For the writer it was moving from the tranquillity of the river's lateral passage in *A Week* to what one biographer called "the blasted, life-threatening wilderness atop Mount Katahdin," and back to the reflective pastoral landscape of his pond at Concord. In *Walden* he would write, "I love the wild not less than the good."[19] To Native Americans the mountain was the sacred precinct of the Algonquin god Pomola. Thoreau noted that "[t]he tops of mountains are among the unfinished parts of the globe, whither it is a slight insult to the gods to climb and pry into their secrets."[20] Scholars have speculated whether he actually reached Katahdin's summit, and his ascent may have been as much imagination as reality. No matter, it was a pure transcending experience, as he exulted with breathless exclamation points: "What is this Titan that has possession of me? Talk of mysteries!—Think of our life in nature,—daily to be shown matter, to come in contact with it,—rocks, trees, wind on our cheeks! the *solid* earth! the *actual* world! the *common sense*! *Contact*! *Contact*!"[21] In turn, the painter had similarly begun to work out this formula of the wild and the good in his paintings of Otter Creek and Newport Mountain. With the addition of the evening sky above Katahdin, he brought his vision to a new level of catharsis.

Church did not return to northern Maine for several years, and when he painted Katahdin again in the 1870s, the mood of the nation and his interpretation of the place were very different. In 1853 he made his first journey to South America and painted a serene view of *Cotopaxi*, 1855 (Smithsonian American Art Museum, Washington, D.C.), in the Andean range of Ecuador. For this canvas he reworked his Katahdin composition, placing a domestic farm scene in the foreground and the snow-covered volcanic peak in the distance. This was also an image of man's harmony with raw primal nature. But it would be at Mount Desert, and to a lesser extent Vermont and New York, where he continued exploration of his sunset iconography.

In 1854 the artist returned to Mount Desert Island and to Nova Scotia. This time he was based in the center of the island, probably at Somes Tavern, one of the earliest lodgings in the area and most likely where Cole had stayed a decade before. Lane had overlapped with Church during several summers at Mount Desert in the early 1850s and had painted a number of views near Somesville. But the Gloucester native had tended to move more by sailboat around the shoreline, whereas Church enjoyed hiking the local pathways and mountain trails. One of the latter's loveliest pencil drawings from

September 1854 is *Road near Somesville* (fig. 35), with its rustling foliage casting mottled patterns of light and shade across the roadway out of town.

Moving off island, he made a number of beautifully refined and spare sketches of the island from the northern end of Frenchman's Bay, including *Mount Desert Island from near Sullivan* (fig. 36) and *Mount Desert Island* (fig. 37). In these he made especially effective use of contrasting passages of charcoal and Chinese white on gray papers for the details of evergreen and cloud shapes. By this time he may have been aware of the growing influence of the English critic John Ruskin's theories of drawing, then just being interpreted and promoted by Church's American contemporary Asher B. Durand in his "Letters on Landscape Painting," appearing in the mid-1850s in *The Crayon*. Ruskin's own manual, *Elements of Drawing*, appeared in 1858 and certainly reinforced Church's natural inclinations toward meticulous rendering of nature's details in his outdoor sketching. Durand had stressed the importance of specificity in recording species of trees and called for capturing "the freedom and air of wildness characteristic of our scenery."[22]

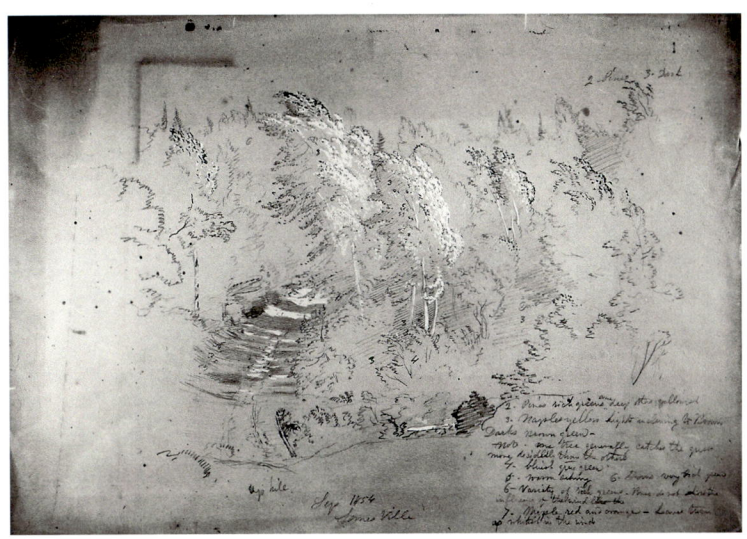

Fig. 35. Frederic Edwin Church, *Road near Somesville, Mount Desert Island*, September 1854, graphite, gouache, and white lead turned black on medium brown paper, 12⅛ × 17⁹⁄₁₆ in., OL.1977.177

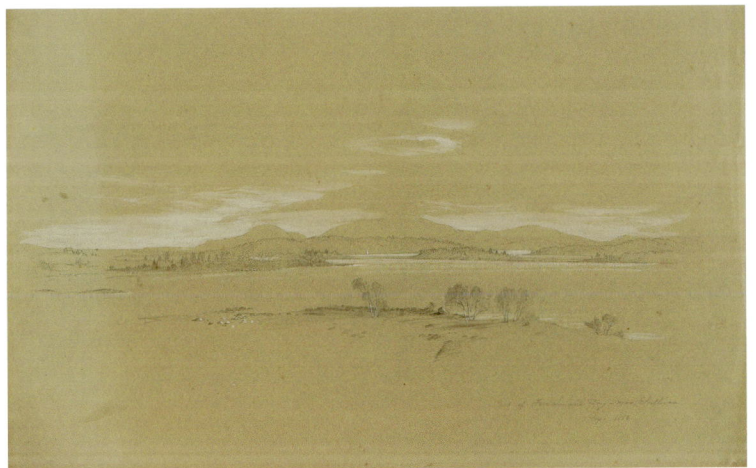

Fig. 36. Frederic Edwin Church, *Mount Desert Island from near Sullivan*, September 1854, graphite, gouache, and white lead on gray-green paper, 10¾ × 17⁵⁄₁₆ in., OL.1980.1459

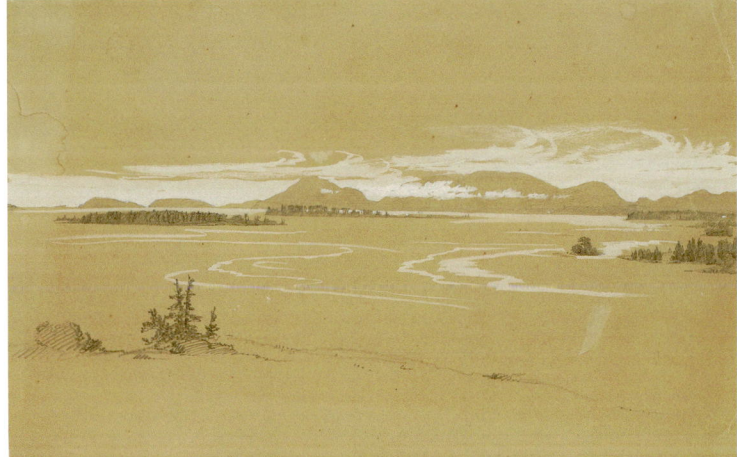

Fig. 37. Frederic Edwin Church, *Mount Desert Island*, c. 1855–56, graphite and gouache on light brown paper, 9³⁄₁₆ × 15 in., OL.1980.1989 recto

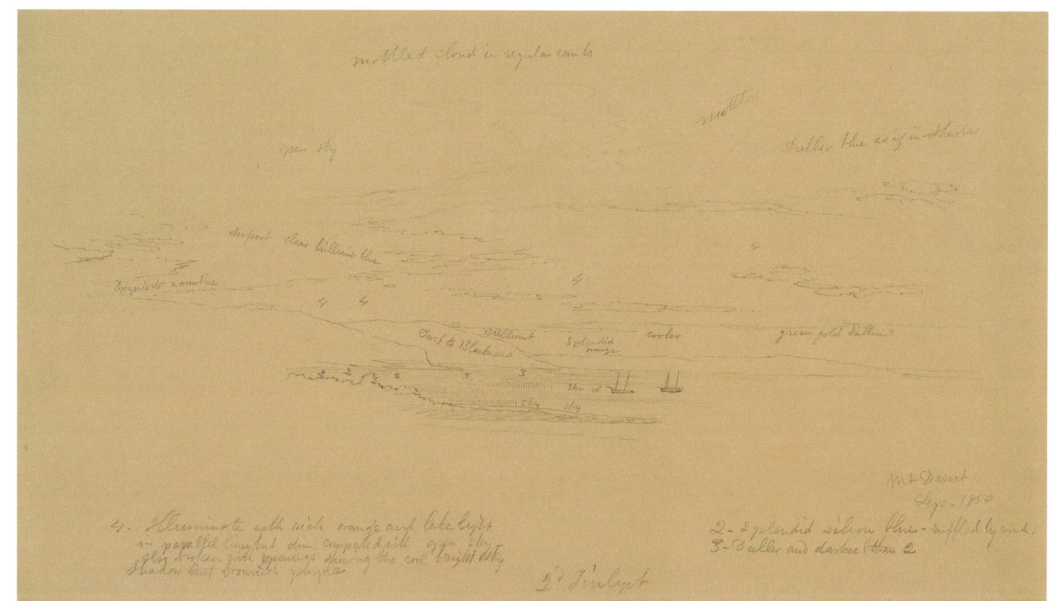

Fig. 38. Frederic Edwin Church, *Sunset, Bar Harbor*, September 1854, graphite on tan paper, 9¹¹⁄₁₆ × 16¹³⁄₁₆ in., OL.1980.1448

Fig. 39. Frederic Edwin Church, *Sunset, Bar Harbor*, c. September 1854, oil on paper mounted on canvas, 10⅛ × 17¼ in., OL.1981.72

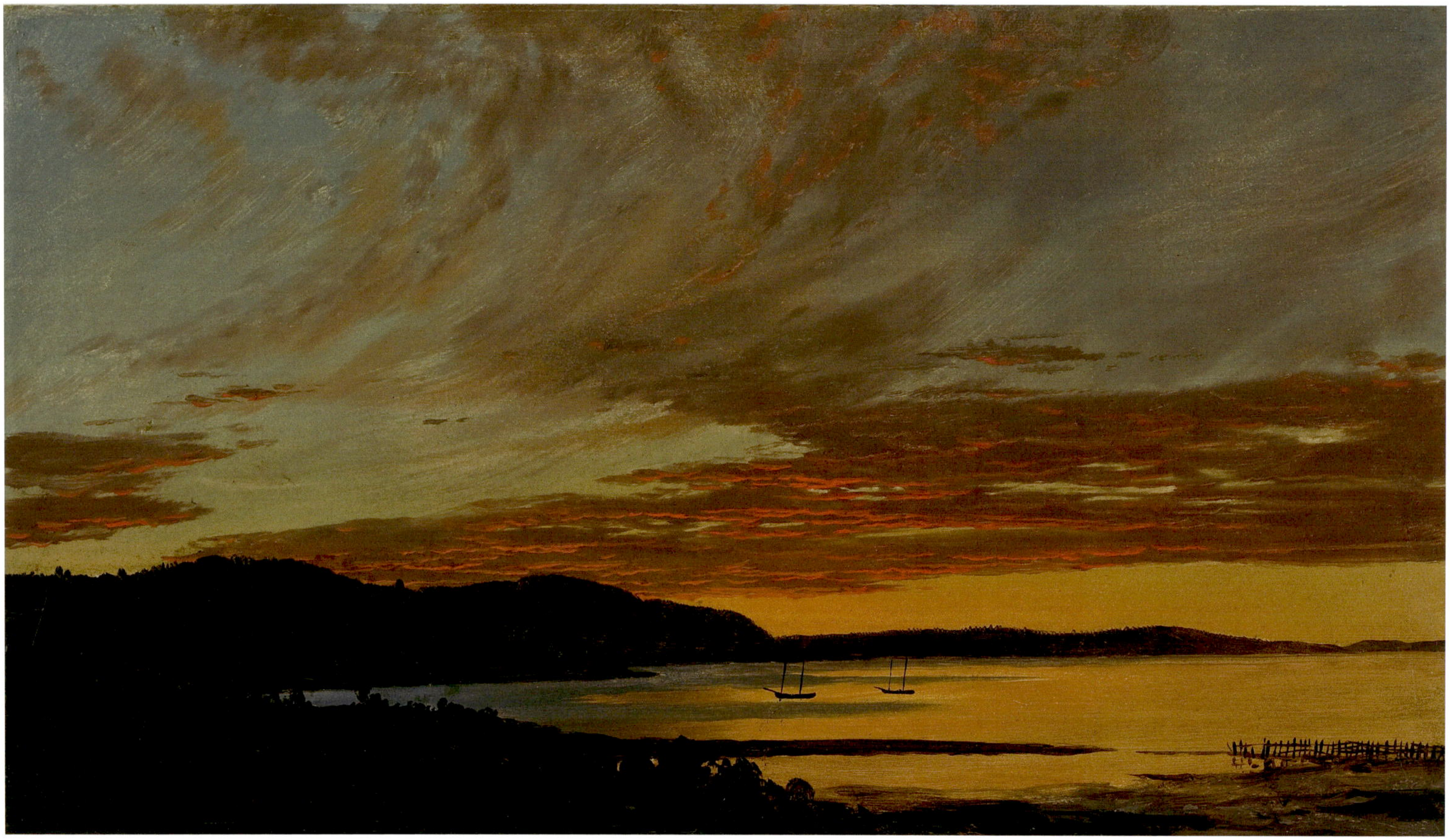

One of his more perfunctory efforts proved to be the most prophetic. *Sunset, Bar Harbor* (fig. 38) outlined a particularly elaborate cloud formation over the island at dusk, on which Church made extensive color notations within the different strata and areas of light, as well as along the lower margin of his sheet. Presumably at the same time he executed a dramatic oil study of the view (fig. 39), in which the cloud outlines are now filled in with the pyrotechnics of intense, reds, yellows, and lavenders. For the time being these were direct recordings of actual experience, and it would take another six years before the artist made use of them to create one of the visionary masterpieces of his career.

Church appears to have been a gregarious colleague and frequently liked to travel with other artists or friends. On his first trip to Mount Desert, fellow painters Regis Gignoux and Richard W. Hubbard joined him; and also on the island that summer were Lane, John F. Kensett, and Benjamin Champney. And appearing in other summers of the 1850s were Albert Bierstadt, William Stanley Haseltine, John Henry Hill, William M. Hart, and Aaron Draper Shattuck.[23] In August and September 1855 Church was part of a large vacationing group of family and friends, organized by Charles Tracy of New York (who later became the father-in-law of J. Pierpont Morgan). Tracy kept a lively diary of their time on the island and provides us with a glimpse of the artist's congenial side, as he was known to sing and play the piano, tell stories, fish, and cook for the group.

Besides Church, the gathering included his close friend Theodore Winthrop plus families with children, twenty-seven in all, this time arriving on the steamer *Rockland*. Over the course of their monthlong stay, there was much hiking and horse and wagon rides. The artist made a couple dozen drawings, several comic caricatures, and cartoon narratives, displaying his clever sense of humor (fig. 40). On August 4 the Tracy log recorded, "Mr. Church says this island is remarkable for fine sunsets; and our stay here is daily proving his impressions just. There cannot be a description of this sunset; it must be seen." Another characteristic entry described one particular day's hike to Eagle Lake:

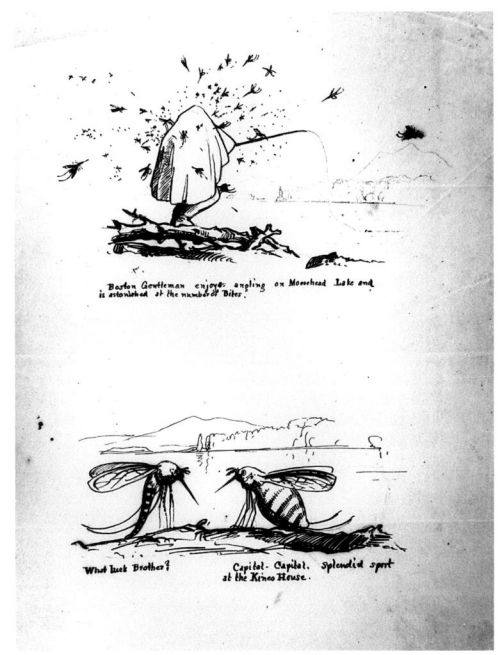

Fig. 40. Frederic Edwin Church, *Two Cartoons*, c. 1852, ink and graphite on thin white paper, 9⅞ × 7¾ in., OL.1980.1601

This lake Mr[.] Church named, from its being so constantly hovered over by eagles. . . . Soon after we turned away, the sun drew near its western plunge, and a tinge of rosy light came upon the bare side of Newport Mountain, turning its whitened and bone like rocks into a beautiful mass of rosy slopes. . . . We soon gained a height from which the sunset itself was visible, and then again we had one of the most superb displays of tinted clouds, and bars of light, over a distant horizon.[24]

Tracy's entries are a mix of serious and comic observations. On the one hand he followed Church in search of pictorial subject matter: "This . . . view greatly resembles the north end of the Highlands as seen from Newburgh. The hills are of similar form and

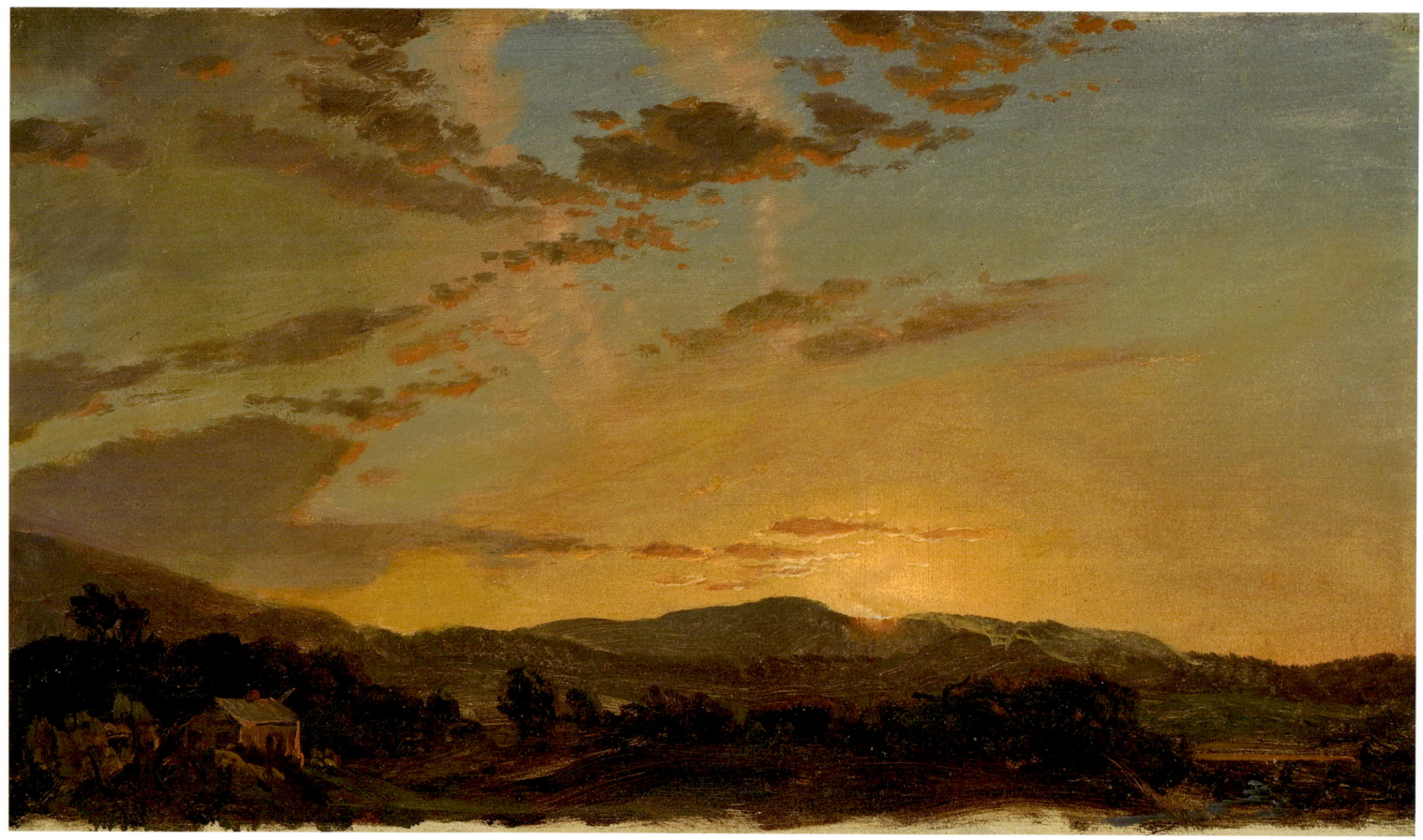

Fig. 41. Frederic Edwin Church, *Maine Sunset*, c. 1856, oil on paper mounted on canvas, 10 × 17½ in., OL.1980.1889

character; and the greater distance in the present case, makes up for the deficiency of height in the Highlands, and equalizes the effect" (figs. 41, 42, and 43). "At dinner table Mr[.] Church announced his design of going today to Schooner Head, to see the beating of the storm on the rocky shore." "Those grand, jagged, independent looking mountains, reaching so far away, and seeming to rise out of the waves, have no equals in interest on the whole coast, if anywhere else." On the other hand were more informal records: "Our evening has gone by blithely. The piano is a standing resource and Mr. Church's capacity for entertainment is perfectly inexhaustible." "Reaching home at supper time, we found Mr. Church had entertained the party hugely by a series of caricature delineations of our operations." "Mr. Church had cut vegetable flowers to ornament the dishes."[25] When the excursion came to an end, the party would "look fondly back to the Mt[.] Desert expedition as the happiest frolic of their lives."[26]

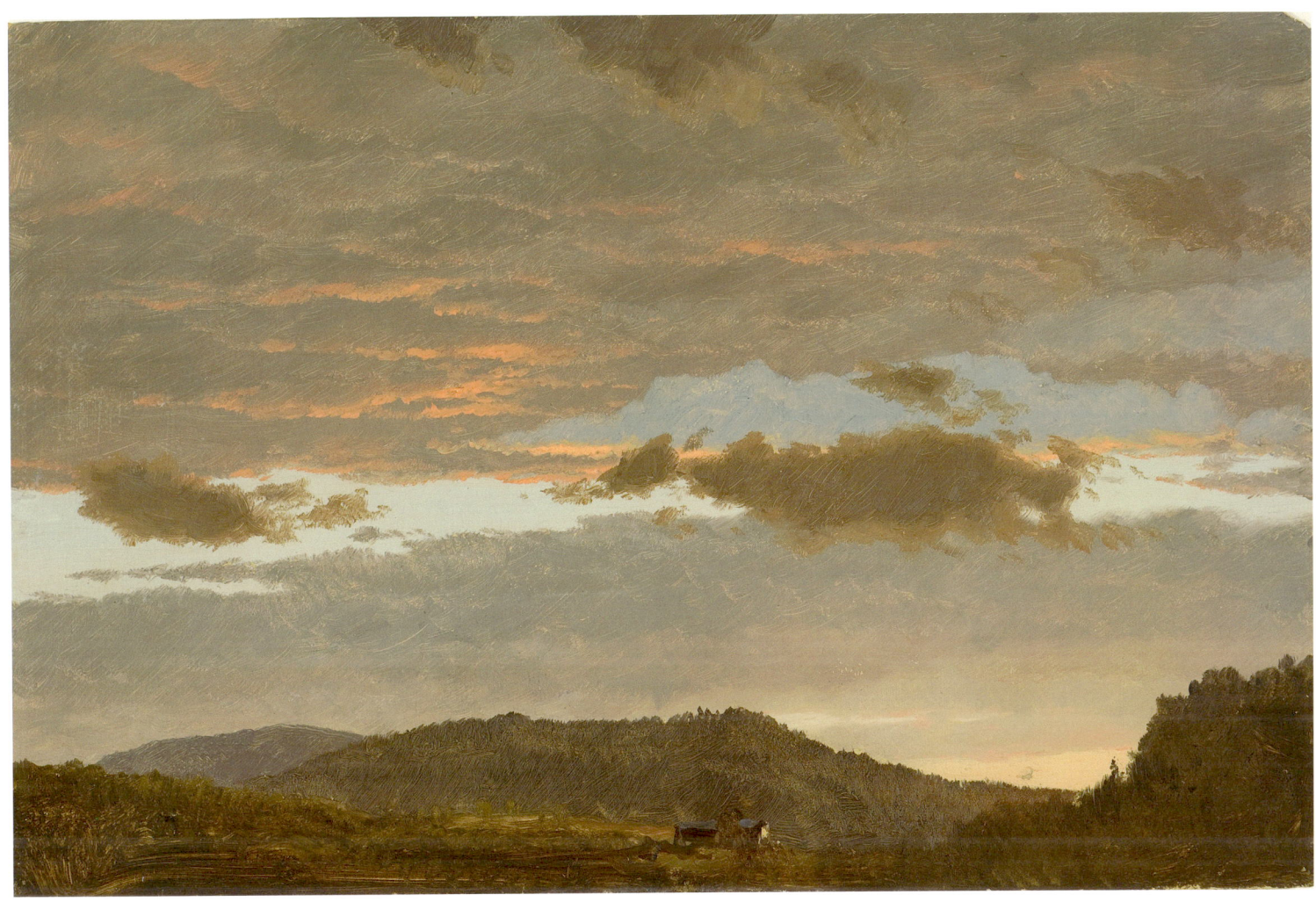

Fig. 42. Frederic Edwin Church, *Maine Twilight*,
c. 1856, oil on heavy buff paper, 11 7/16 × 17 9/16 in.,
OL.1978.12

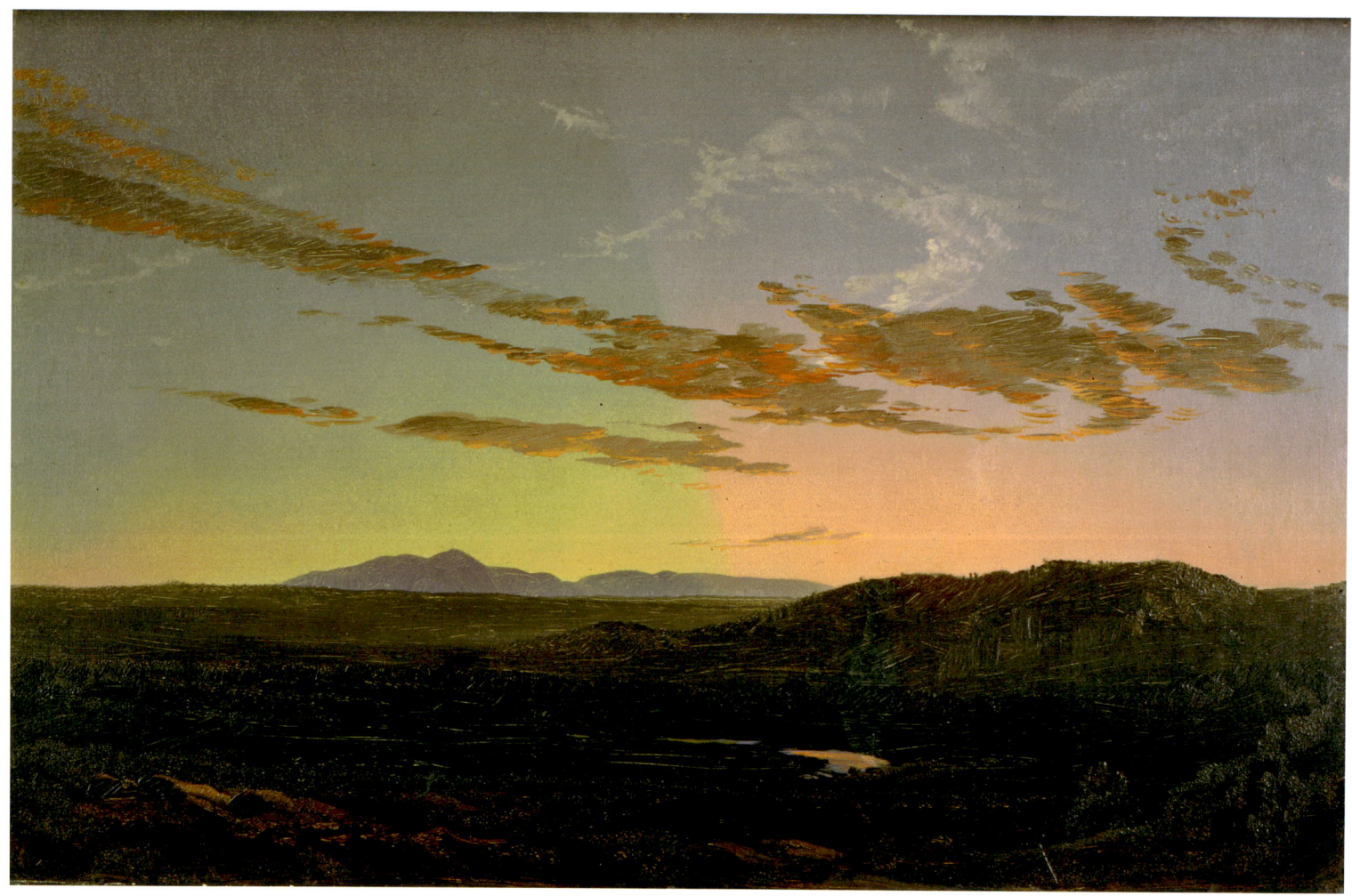

Fig. 43. Frederic Edwin Church, *Sunset*, c. 1856–65, oil on paper mounted on ragboard and panel, 11⅝ × 18¼ in., OL.1980.1633

The mood of the country was moving in a different direction, as issues of race and states' rights were becoming increasingly tense. The failure of the Wilmot Proviso in 1849, the ill-fated Compromise of 1850, leading a few years later to the Kansas-Nebraska Act and Bleeding Kansas, were accumulating evidence of internal national conflict. One of the ways Church would respond to this growing turbulence was to explore his artistic vocabulary. Painting hot cadmium sunsets proved to be the perfect emotional outlet. In 1856 he traveled with Tracy and Winthrop from the Adirondacks through the White Mountains to Mount Desert and on to Mount Katahdin. Winthrop kept an account this time, "Life in the Open Air, and Other Papers," which was published in 1863 after his death in the Civil War. "We both needed to be somewhere near the heart of New England's wildest wilderness. We needed to see Katahdin, —the distinctest mountain to be found on this side of the continent." They camped at Abol

Deadwater at the mouth of Abol Stream, where it joins the Penobscot River. "We turned from sunshine and Cosmos into fog and chaos." Church made sketches of twilight from the mountain summit as well as more distant views of the peak in evening colors. These were reworkings of his 1853 canvas, but gaining in intensity as if in search of a new national statement. "After camps at Katahdin any residence in the woods without a stupendous mountain before the door would have been tame."[27]

One very important canvas to result from this return visit he simply titled *Sunset* (fig. 44). It is among the most beautiful yet haunting of Church's entire twilight series. In contrast to previous works, it seems to have a more nuanced palette, with undertones of anxiety rather than elegy. It feels specific in location but remains ambiguous in identification. Two elements contribute to this change in mood. First, the tonality of the whole is more somber with the shadowed foreground and aged isolated pine and darkened reds of the sky. The juxtaposition of orange-red and lemon yellow in the distance is unusually sharp, while the lavender and dirty yellow of the lake's reflection has a near acidic quality, giving a disturbing edge to the scene's beauty. Second, Church has introduced a new generalization and universality into this wilderness vista. We don't know exactly where this is. The foreground lake looks like Mount Desert, most likely Eagle Lake, whereas the distant pointed peak is not one of the rounded hills on the island, but more suggestive of Katahdin. It is as if Church wanted to conflate coastal and inland Maine in a new summary of American nature. Given its date, we have to wonder if this is his first

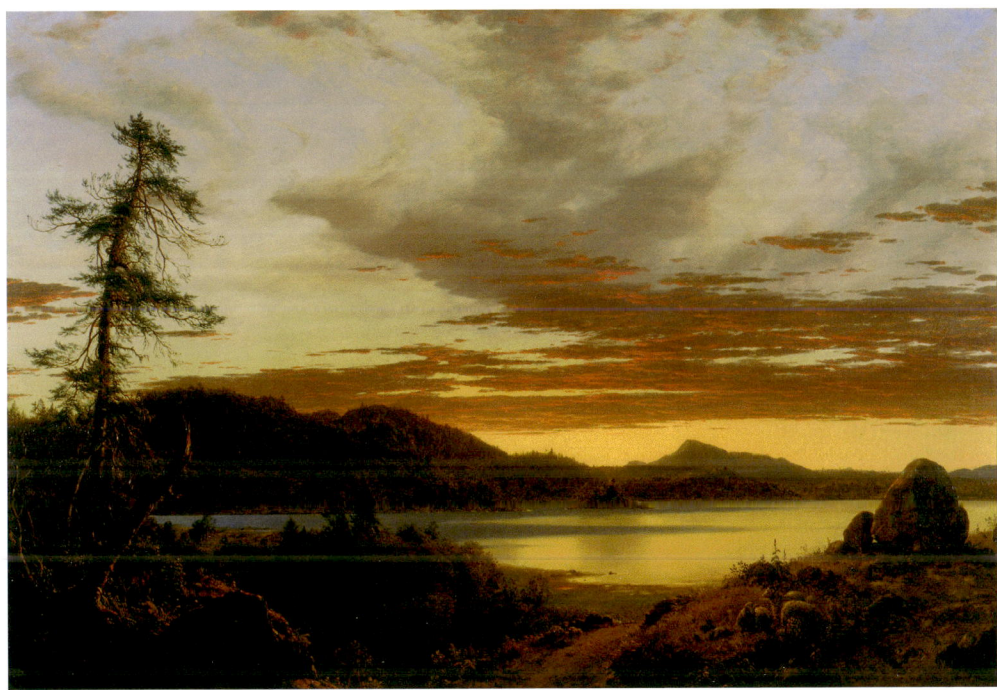

Fig. 44. Frederic Edwin Church, *Sunset*, 1856, oil on canvas, 24 × 36 in., Munson-Williams-Proctor Arts Institute, Utica, Proctor Collection, PC.21. Image courtesy Munson-Williams-Proctor Arts Institute/ Art Resource, NY

intuitive rendering of the heightened national tension as the approach of strife began to seem inevitable.

The fact is that Church undertook nearly a dozen large canvases and smaller oil studies of twilight scenery during the later 1850s. A number of these depicted inland settings either in upstate New York or Vermont, as well as additional sketches of Katahdin.[28] We should also remember that in this same period he was visiting South America and Niagara, also the subjects of major works. As an aside, it is worth noting that most of his Andean pictures from these years tended to be of sunrise or clear midday, as if a reflection of a greater optimism and spiritual purity he found in the tropical wilderness. When he did return to his final great Maine sunset in 1860, the nation was on the threshold of civil war, and almost all scholarship on Church sees *Twilight in the Wilderness* (see fig. 1) as emblematic of this explosive moment.

David Huntington, Church's first modern biographer, said the painting "was the natural apocalypse" and declared, "the sky is the hour's anticipated Archangel, come to proclaim 'a great turning point.'" In further biblical language, he announced this a Day of Judgment.[29] To Franklin Kelly it was "an eloquent pictorial plea for wilderness preservation . . . enacting the struggle to save some vestige of the primeval, natural American land." But "there was, of course, an even more explosive issue facing America during the 1850s . . . slavery." On another occasion Kelly added that the work reflected "Church's uneasiness about the future of his country."[30] In a subsequent monograph John K. Howat deemphasizes the historical associations of the picture in favor of its coloristic triumph and its insight into the threatened state of the national wilderness: it "so successfully conveys the feeling of undefiled and glorious nature of an America that was beginning to experience man's rough embrace."[31]

Three primary aspects are dominant in this pivotal picture: the meteorological, the spiritual, and the national. This particular cloud formation reflecting the setting sun is several thousands of feet high in the atmosphere, what weather reporters today would describe as a sharp front about to bring impending change. From its configuration we know Church in part worked from his pencil drawing and oil study of a sunset he saw at Bar Harbor in 1854 (see figs. 38 and 39). But something triggered this much more intense, even lurid, version a few years later. Scholars have argued that he witnessed a notably brilliant occurrence, specifically during the summer solstice of June 21–22, 1858, and undertook new sketches that led to work on the final canvas (fig. 45). A year later he also probably witnessed the powerful display of northern lights that were visible in New England from late August through the first days of September.[32] Some have suggested that this brilliant phenomenon was another harbinger of change, though Church did not develop a large canvas of the subject until 1865, when it took on a quite different meaning.

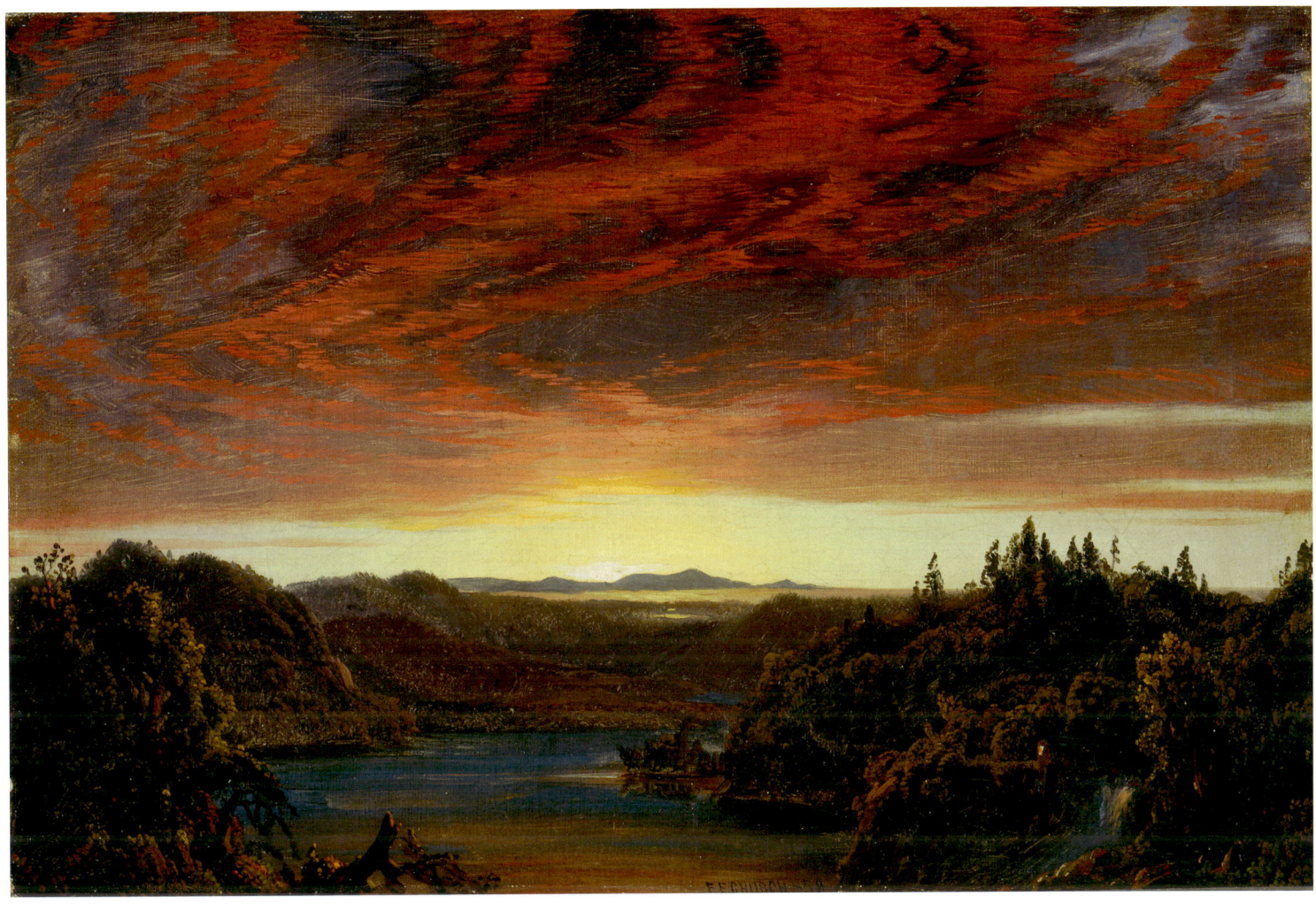

Fig. 45. Frederic Edwin Church, *Twilight,
A Sketch*, 1858, oil on canvas, 8¼ × 12¼ in.,
OL.1981.8

Tied to the meteorological display was the artist's strong religious faith. He presents
the landscape as a day of judgment. On the right side three trees appear in various stages
of decay and collapse within this primeval forest, signifying the cycle of time. We have
seen previously how Church introduced cross-shaped imagery in his compositions. (He
also frequently included white steeples in several early landscapes, visual signatures of
his name but equally emblems of God's presence in nature.) Prominent in the foreground
of *Twilight in the Wilderness* is a large decayed tree stump (see fig. 1). If we look closely,
the configuration of broken branches reads as a figure praying before a cross. It is hard
to assess here whether we are witnessing a crisis of faith or the hope for redemption.
We need to remember that in addition to the imminence of national strife, in the year
before Church completed his painting Charles Darwin's *On the Origin of Species* was published, creating an intellectual assault of profound magnitude. It sold out in Britain and

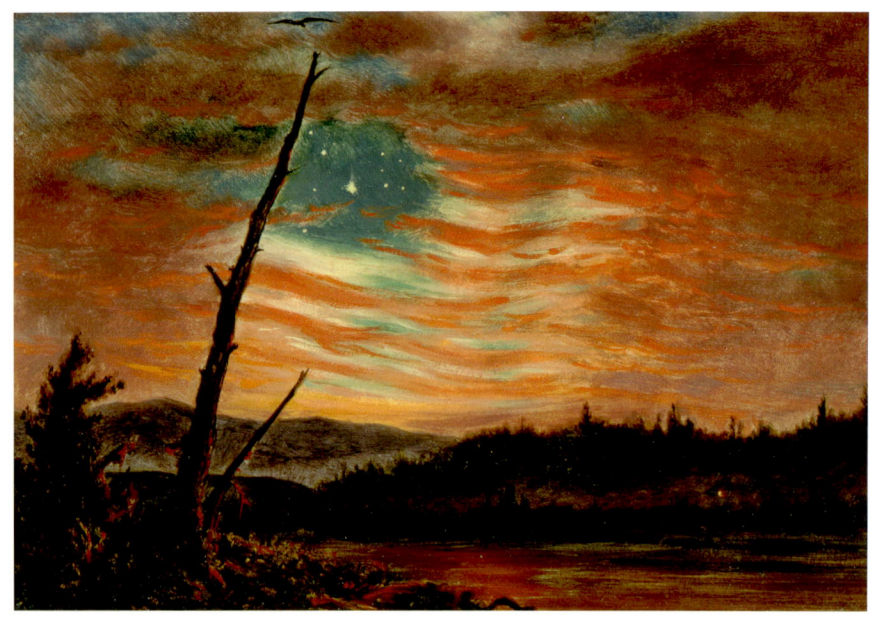

America within a matter of months, and Church was certainly familiar with it. Darwin showed how natural history was cruel and haphazard, and by implication not divinely ordered and sustained. Such ideas directly undermined the premises of Hudson River landscape painting to this point, and Church's vision seems to embrace this spiritual conflict as well.

One key change he made in moving from his sketches to the final painting was to universalize the setting. Howat has suggested it could have shown possible views of a lake in the Katahdin region, and most historians agree that it remains a Maine subject, but that it now expands to become a continental landscape, pertinent to the state of the nation. We know this from explicit details and intentional visual associations. At the far left silhouetted against the sky sitting atop a barren tree is an eagle, symbol of the nation and witness to this apocalyptic moment. In addition, the next year Church painted a small canvas, also replicated in a color lithograph, called *Our Banner in the Sky* (fig. 46), which recast the flaming sunset into a tattered American flag flying from a shorn tree trunk.[33] We know Church came from an ardent Union family, and after the outbreak of war, his next major canvas was *The Icebergs*, 1861 (Dallas Museum of Art), which he retitled *The North* for its debut and a lithographed version. Moreover, prominent in its foreground are the remains of a lost ship in the Arctic, the cross-shaped form of a broken mast and crow's nest lying on the ice.

With this culminating work, Church was nearing the end of his interest and depictions of Mount Desert. His last recorded visits were in September 1860 and in 1862. There were a few other strong oil studies of light effects on the island that he executed during the later 1850s, such as *Eagle Lake Viewed from Cadillac Mountain* (fig. 47), with the afternoon sun reflecting across distant passages of water to the west and blazing on the surface of the lake below us. This central axis of vertical light was one of Church's many nods to the work of James M. W. Turner. Another striking oil sketch viewed the *Moon Rising over Porcupine Islands, Bar Harbor* (fig. 48), c. 1860, with an aura of fog filling the gray-blue sky over the Porcupine Islands. One last major canvas dates from 1865, mostly a memory image of the island seen from far off, its profile generalized and the sun now the glowing embers of expiration (fig. 49). He had largely exhausted the vocabulary and symbolism of this coastal terrain and turned to different locales to mark the passage of the war years.

Fig. 46. Unknown engraver, chromolithograph, published by Goupil & Co, New York, 1861, oil over chromolithograph, after Frederic Edwin Church, *Our Banner in the Sky* (April–May 1861), 7⁹⁄₁₆ × 11⅜ in., OL.1976.29

Fig. 47. Frederic Edwin Church, *Eagle Lake Viewed from Cadillac Mountain, Mount Desert Island, Maine*, c. 1850–60, oil and graphite on paperboard, 11⁹⁄₁₆ × 17½ in., Cooper-Hewitt National Design Museum, Smithsonian Institution, New York, Gift of Louis P. Church, 1917-4-324. Photograph: Matt Flynn, Image Courtesy Cooper-Hewitt National Design Museum/Art Resource, NY

Fig. 48. Frederic Edwin Church, *Moon Rising over Porcupine Islands, Bar Harbor*, c. 1860, oil on paperboard, 5½ × 11⅞ in., Cooper-Hewitt National Design Museum, Smithsonian Institution, New York, Gift of Louis P. Church, 1917-4-1355. Photograph: Matt Flynn, Image Courtesy Cooper-Hewitt National Design Museum/Art Resource, NY

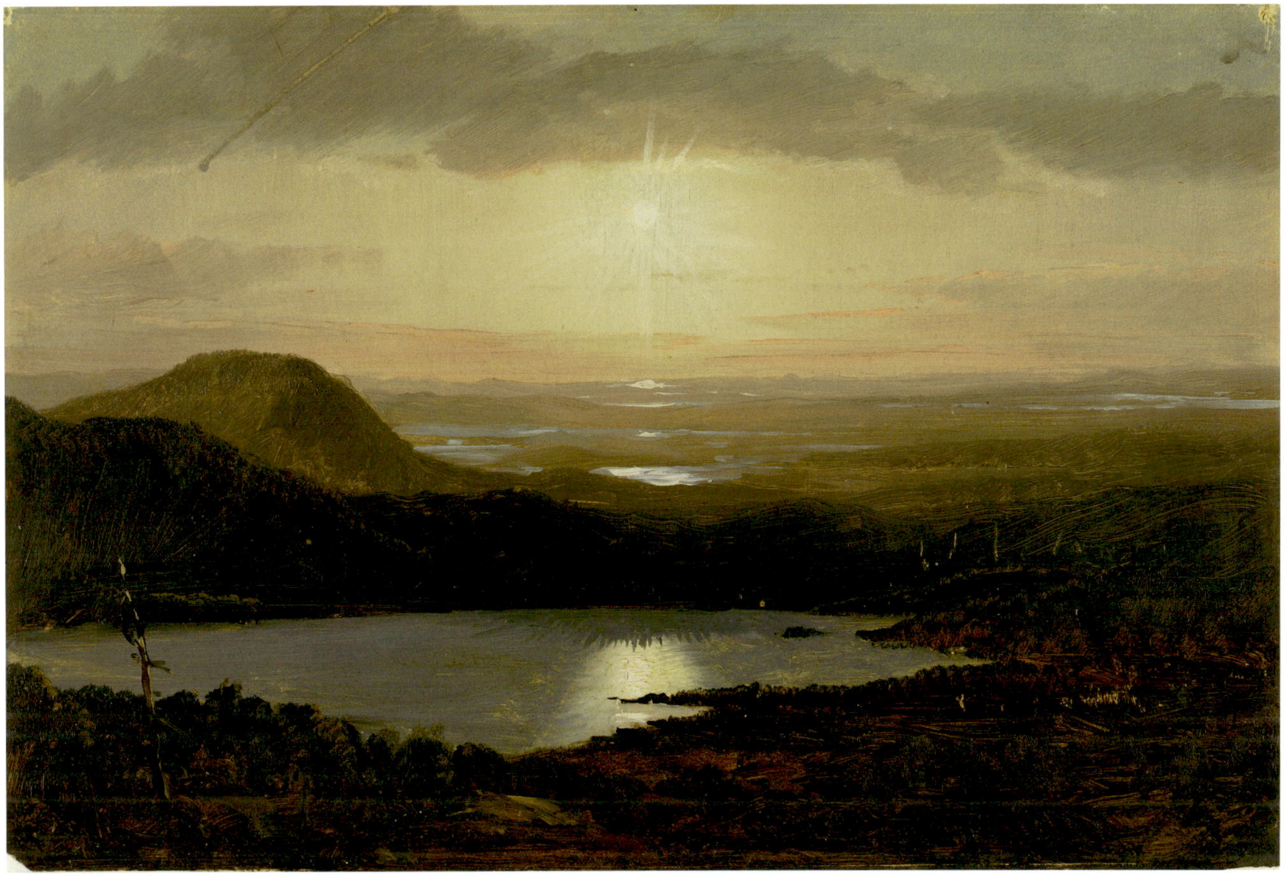

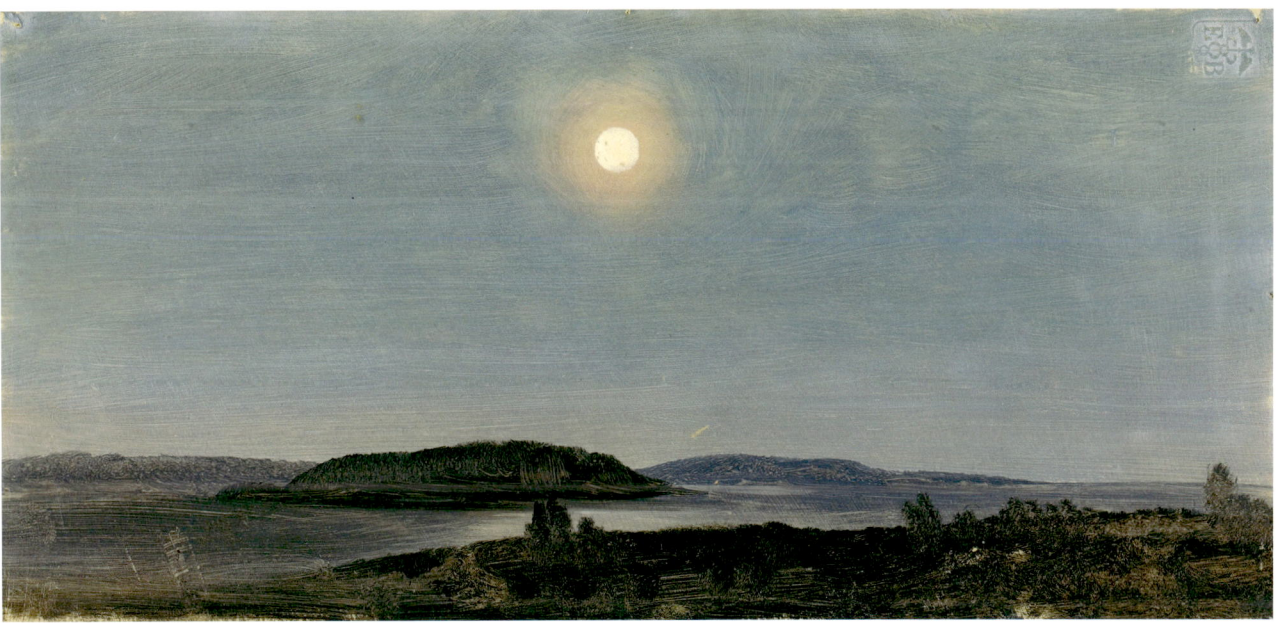

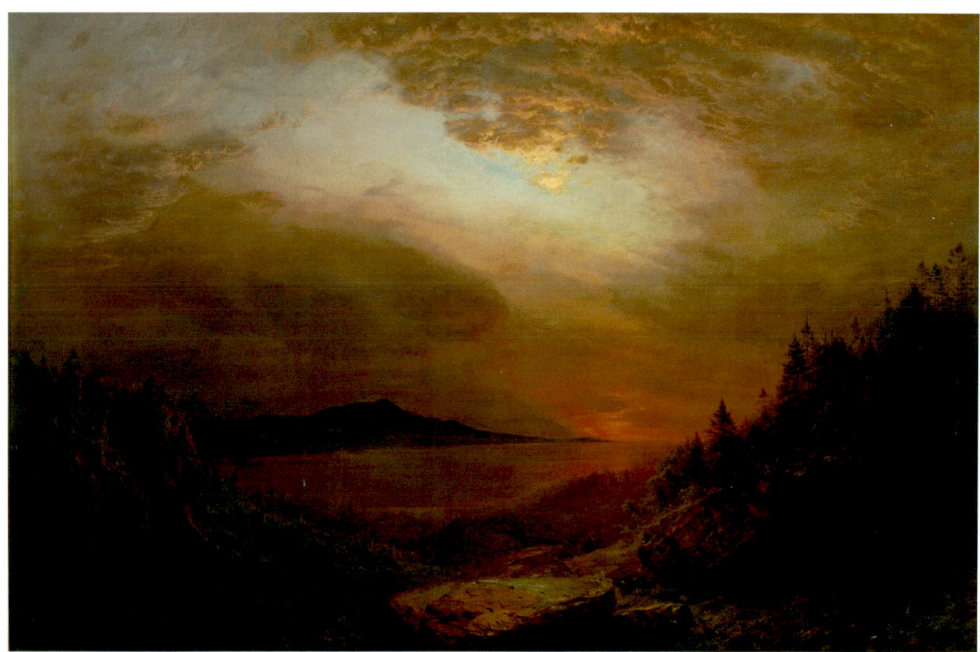

Fig. 49. Frederic Edwin Church, *Twilight: Mount Desert Island, Maine*, 1865, oil on canvas, 31⁵⁄₁₆ × 48⁷⁄₁₆ in., Mildred Lane Kemper Art Museum, Washington University, St. Louis, Bequest of Charles Parsons, 1905, WU2175

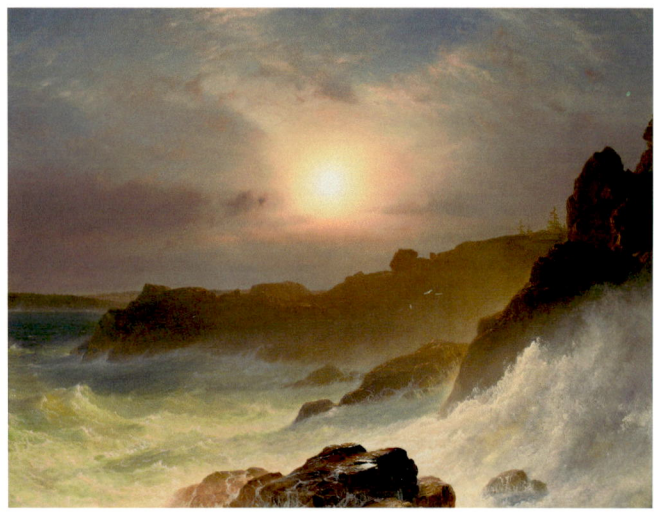

Fig. 50. Frederic Edwin Church, *Coast Scene, Mount Desert*, 1863, oil on canvas, 36⅛ × 48 in., Wadsworth Atheneum Museum of Art, Hartford, Bequest of Mrs. Clara Hinton Gould, 1948.178

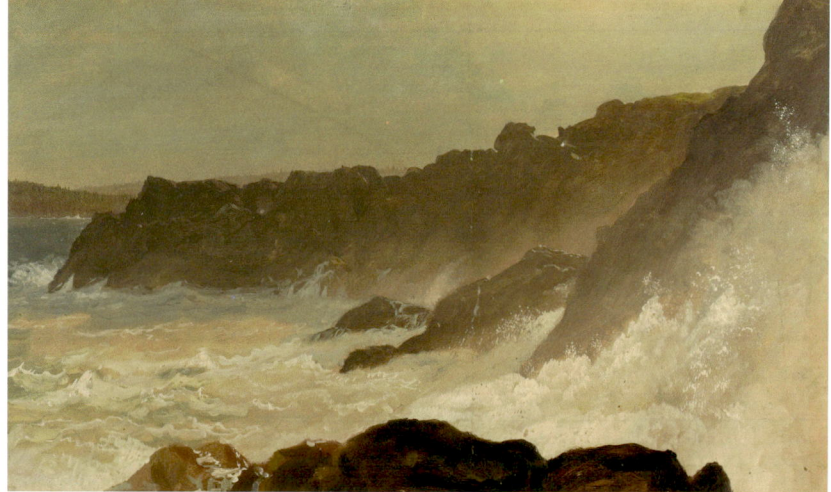

Fig. 51. Frederic Edwin Church, *Surf Pounding against the Rocky Maine Coast*, 1862, oil and graphite on thin paperboard, 11¾ × 20 in., Cooper-Hewitt National Design Museum, Smithsonian Institution, New York, Gift of Louis P. Church, 1917-4-1324. Photograph: Matt Flynn, Image Courtesy Cooper-Hewitt National Design Museum/Art Resource, NY

The 1862 visit did yield one powerful painting, appropriately a turbulent storm scene showing surf crashing on the island's south coast. With the rocky shore to our right and open water at the left, we are looking toward the west, where an afternoon sun is nearly obscured by the stormy clouds (fig. 50).[34] Church made a detailed oil study of the surf in preparation (fig. 51). The resulting painting exaggerates the treacherous cliffs, and adds the struggle of light and atmosphere in the upper half. It almost possesses the ominous mystery of an eclipse, with the battle of water and rock conveying a very different mood from the pastoral sublime Church had painted a few years before (see fig. 50). Similarly, his 1862 version of *Cotopaxi* (The Detroit Institute of Arts) replaced the cool serenity of his 1855 view, with the volcano now exploding in violent combat with the sun itself, the earth and cosmos erupting in liquid fire. His landscapes continued to respond to the trauma of the war up until its conclusion. He marked its end with *Aurora Borealis*, 1865 (fig. 52), in which an iridescent spectrum of colors arcs across the Arctic sky, and further celebrated the idea of national union the following year with *Rainy Season in the Tropics*, 1866 (Fine Arts Museums of San Francisco), where a radiant double rainbow sweeps over a deep mountainous ravine, binding together the two sides of the landscape within. With these works Church's practice of landscape as history painting had run its course. Moreover, after his visit of 1862, he would not return to Maine for another decade and a half, and then it would be only to Mount Katahdin for five out of six years in the later 1870s through early 1880s.

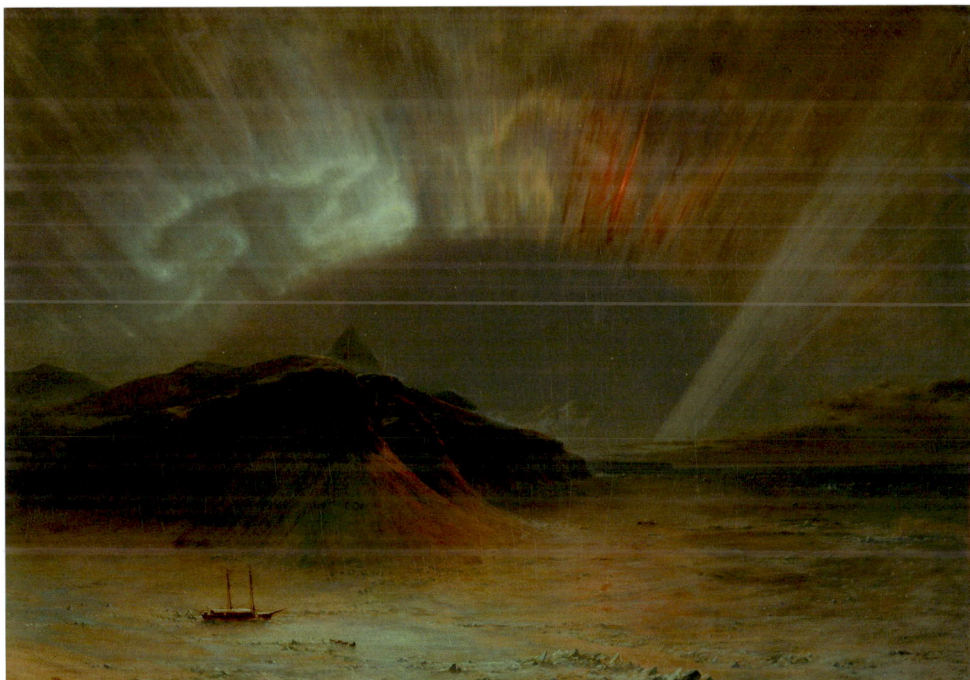

Fig. 52. Frederic Edwin Church, *Aurora Borealis*, 1865, oil on canvas, 56⅛ × 83½ in., Smithsonian American Art Museum, Washington, D.C., 1911.4.1. Image Courtesy Smithsonian American Art Museum/Art Resource, NY

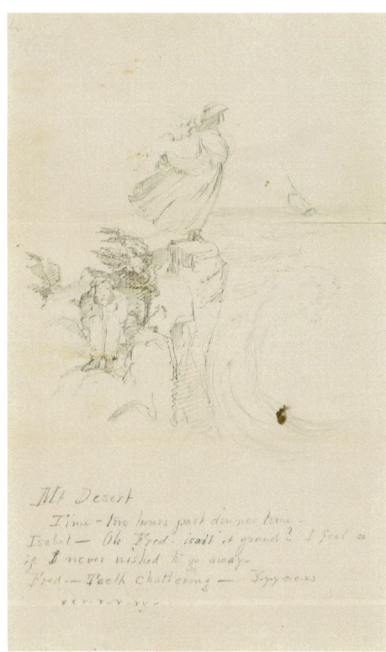

Fig. 53. Frederic Edwin Church, *Frederic and Isabel Church at Mount Desert Island*, c. 1860–62, graphite on thin white wove paper, 8 × 5 in., OL.1980.1603

There were several interrelated reasons for this. As we have seen, the events of the national agony were over. Nature as a manifestation of God's hand had been challenged. The heroic landscape seemed less in tune with the changed circumstances of the country as it entered a new period of industrialization, internationalism, and immigration. By the 1870s graver forms of realism began to emerge with a younger generation of painters like Winslow Homer, Thomas Eakins, and Eastman Johnson. Gradually, the grand salon canvases of Church and his rival in western landscape, Albert Bierstadt, started to go out of favor for being romantic and histrionic. Importantly, Church's personal life and energies now shifted in other directions. He had married in 1860, and family affairs soon took more attention, with his first two children born in 1862 and 1864 (fig. 53). In celebration he painted small companion canvases, *Sunrise* and *Moonrise* (both at Olana State Historic Site). That joy was dashed the following year with the deaths of both from diphtheria. It is conceivable that he saw the transcendent lighting in *Aurora Borealis* at this time as having private memorial associations. In any case, this was a moment in his art of turning from public to personal meanings.

Four more children were born over the next few years, as domestic life took hold, and in 1860 Church purchased a farm near Hudson, New York, where he built a cottage. Over the next years he added to the property and in 1867 purchased the hilltop with the intent of building a more substantial home. Construction of the Persian-Italianate villa on the property he later named Olana was underway between 1870 and 1872 (figs. 54 and 55). But the later 1860s also saw the artist undertake a major trip through the Middle East and Europe, which resulted in important canvases of *Jerusalem from the Mount of Olives*, 1870 (Nelson-Atkins Museum, Kansas City), *The Parthenon*, 1870 (The Metropolitan Museum of Art), and *El Khasné, Petra*, 1874 (Olana State Historic Site). The building of the house, one of the most unusual and spectacular artist homes surviving in America, became a work of art in its own right. Church blended eastern and western elements into its detailing and filled the house with artifacts collected abroad (see fig. 55). Besides his own works and those by friends on the walls, he designed the views from major windows, terraces, and balconies to frame living landscape compositions (figs. 56 and 57). Thus domestic life and space drew his principal emotional and creative drives during these years.

It may have been that Church now recalled his earlier travels to the Mount Katahdin area, possibly associating his own manipulated landscape of water and woodlands at Olana with the juxtaposition of lakes and ponds, like Togue, Chimney, and Millinocket, adjacent to the Maine mountain. In 1876 he traveled with the Bangor photographer James C. Stodder, who recorded their camping locations and activities in the northern Maine woods. A year later Church decided to return to the area, and in 1878 A. L. Holley wrote an account of a visit with Sanford Gifford and other painter friends, published in

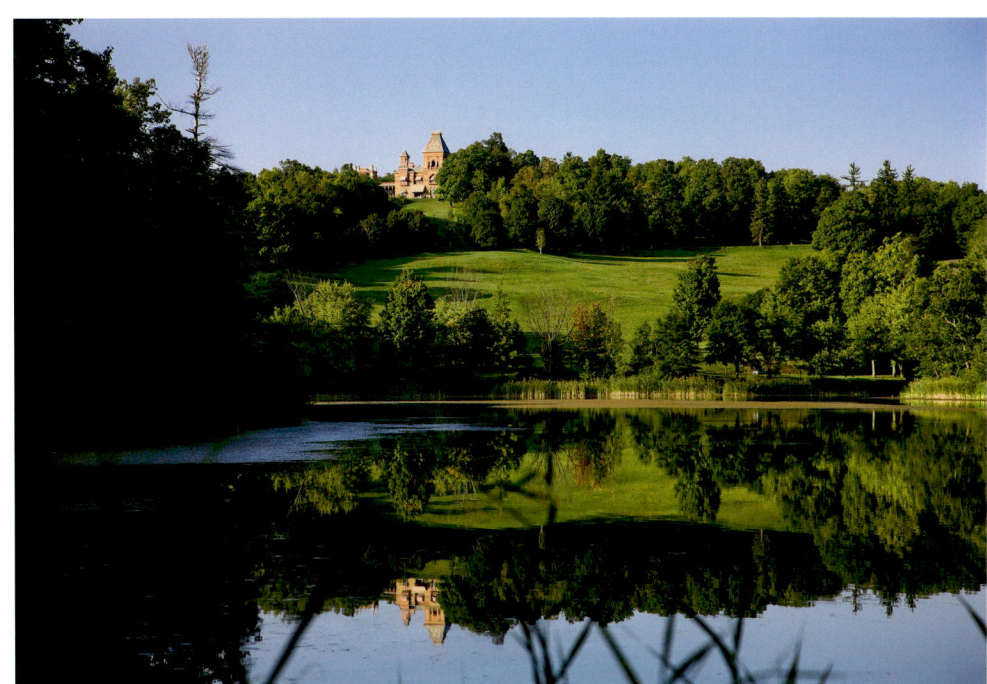

Fig. 54. Peter Aaron, *View across the Lake, Olana*, photograph, 2010, #2010A53.442. © Peter Aaron/Esto.

Fig. 55. Peter Aaron, *Court Hall, Olana*, photograph, 2010, #2010A53.438. © Peter Aaron/Esto.

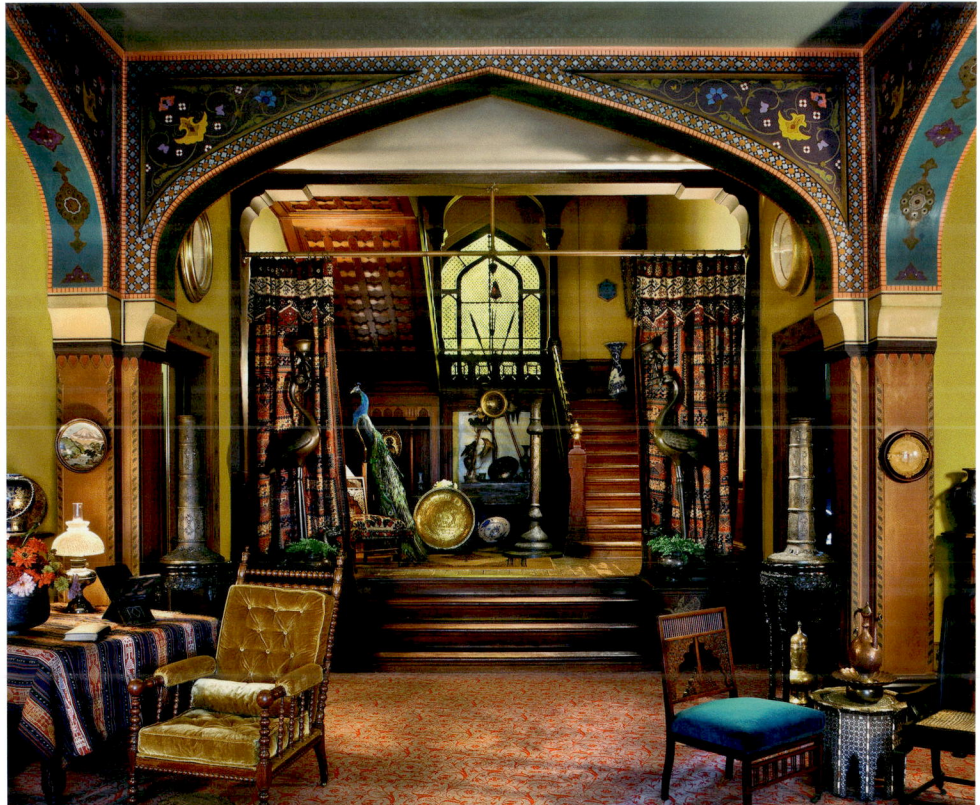

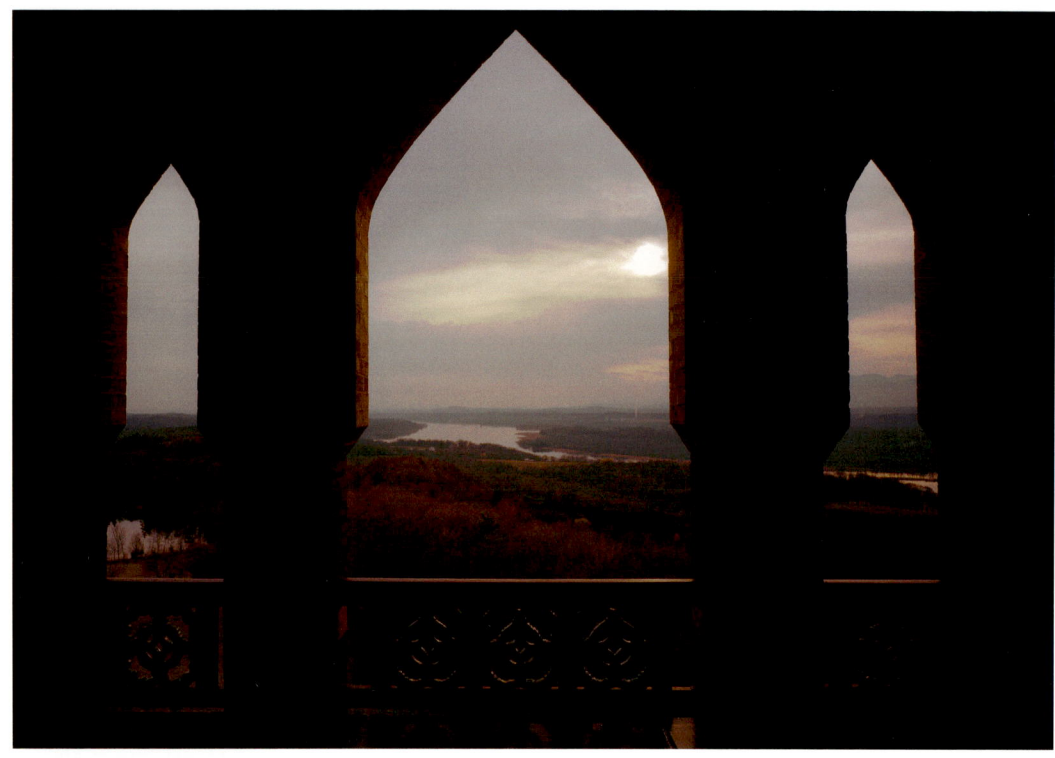

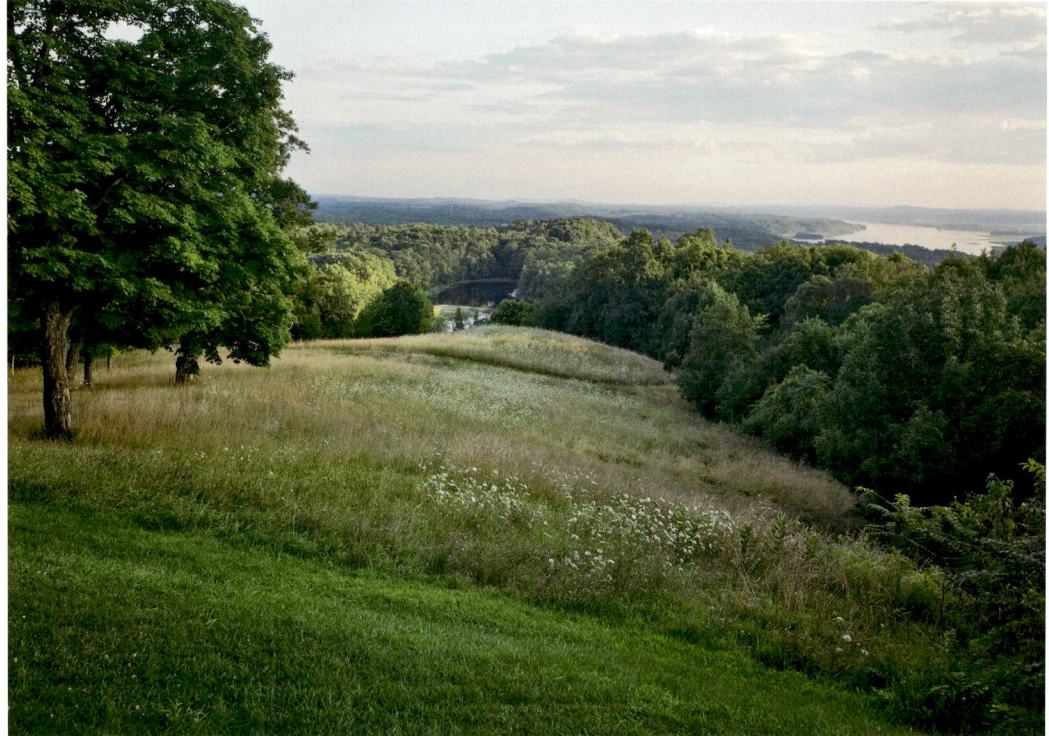

Fig. 57. Larry Lederman, *View Down to the Lake and Beyond to the Hudson, Olana*, photograph, 2010

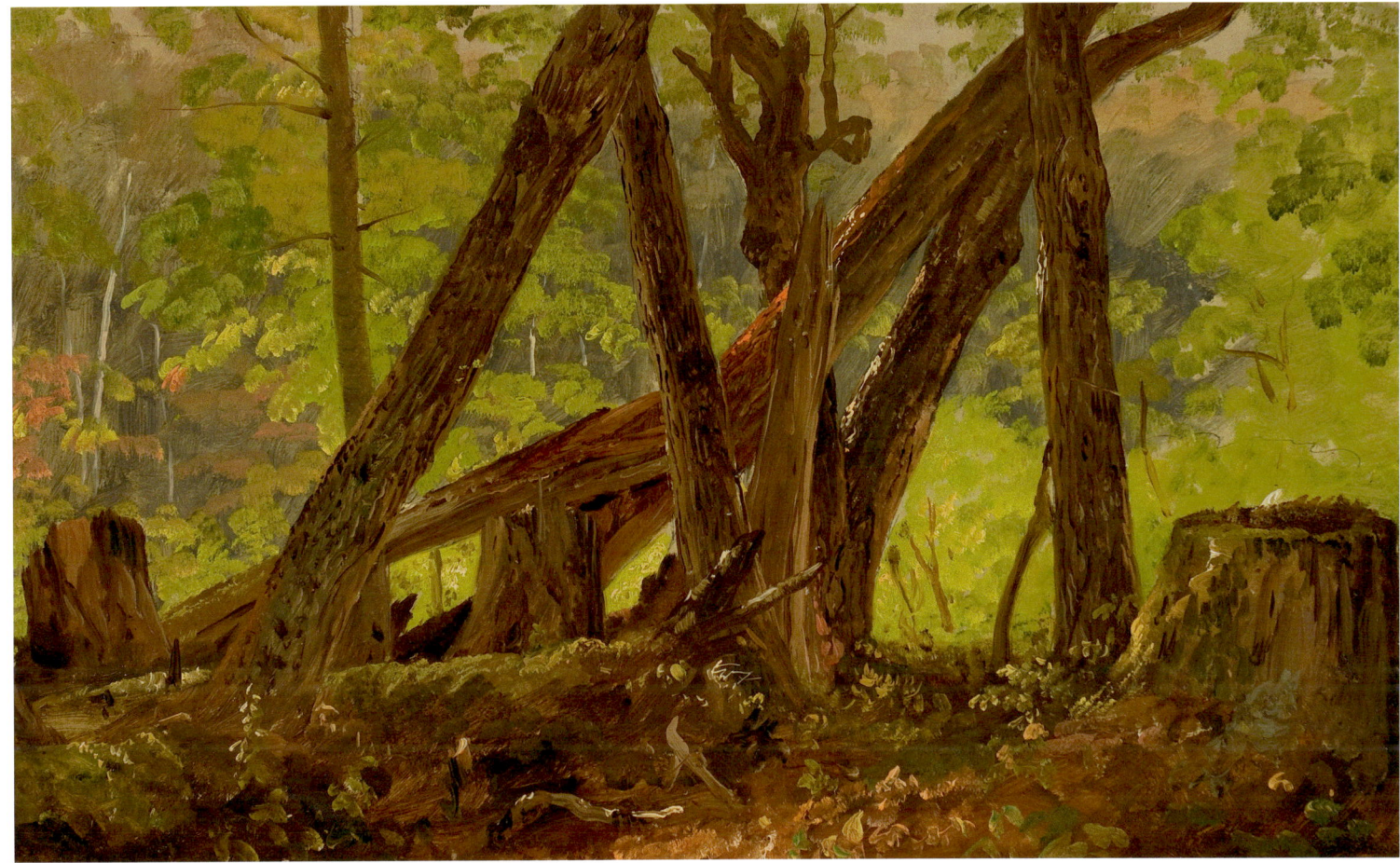

Fig. 58. Frederic Edwin Church, *Wood Interior on Mount Turner*, c. 1877, oil and graphite on paper mounted on canvas, 12⅝₁₆ × 20⅝₁₆ in., OL.1980.1869

Scribner's Monthly as "Camps and Tramps about Ktaadn."[35] Unlike his trips in the early 1850s, these later visits were more recreational than adventurous. The mountain was more an attraction for sportsmen than an experience of primeval wilderness. Camping had now become popular, part of the national obsession with sports, and inland Maine received promotion from the Boston & Maine and Maine Central Railroads.[36] Church's party made their way in by canoe and pack sleds. He mixed climbing, fishing, and hiking with sketching in the woods and across the lake to the peak (fig. 58). Like the Tracy group at Mount Desert two decades earlier, the artist cooked and actively participated in camp life (fig. 59). He was "still the same faithful student of nature, beguiles the leisure hours with innumerable stories and jokes," reported Holley.[37]

The artist purchased the fifty-acre Stevens Farm on the south shore of Millinocket Lake in 1878, which brought him back for successive stays. The property gave him unobstructed views across the water to the mountain, and he repeatedly sketched it and the surrounding woods in pencil and oil studies (figs. 60, 61, and 62). "Go to the

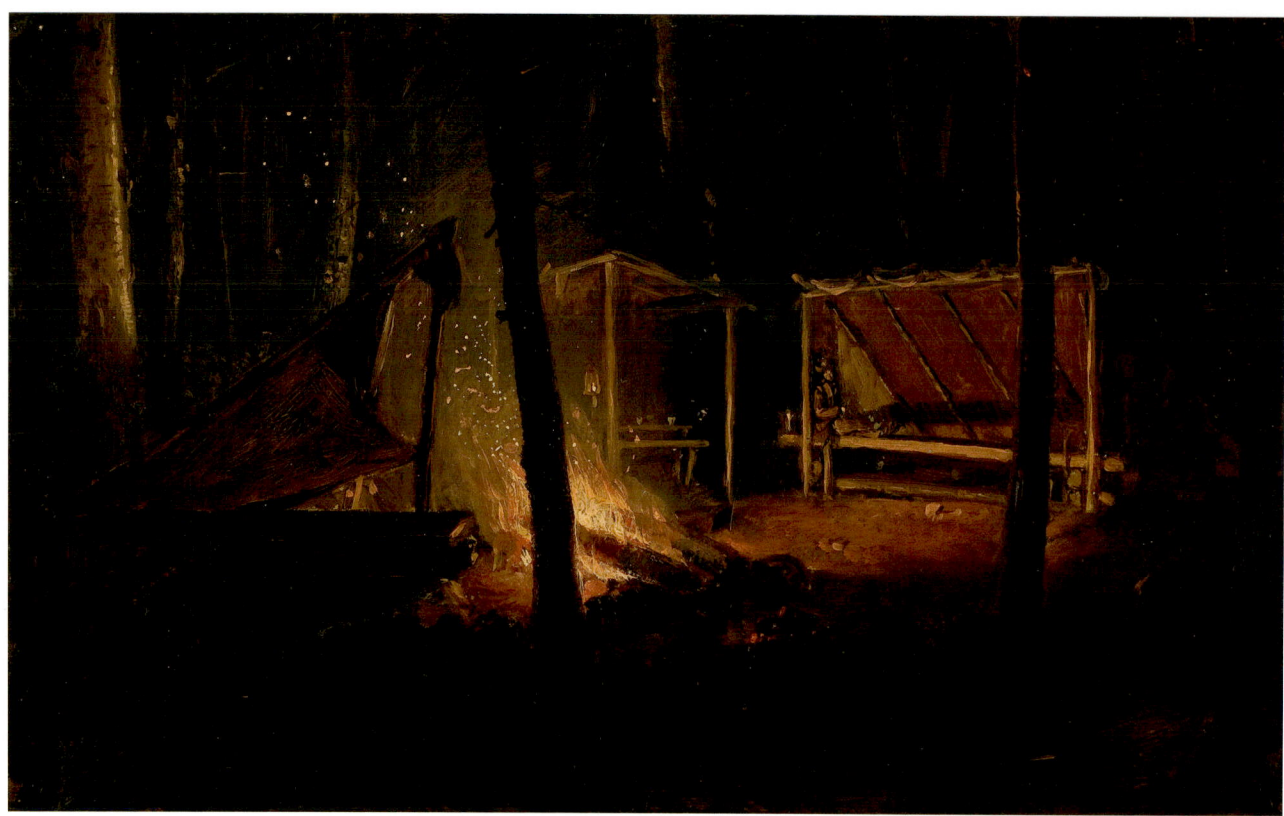

Fig. 59. Frederic Edwin Church, *Campfire near Mount Katahdin*, c. 1877,
oil on paper mounted on canvas, 12⅜ × 20⅜ in., OL.1980.1916

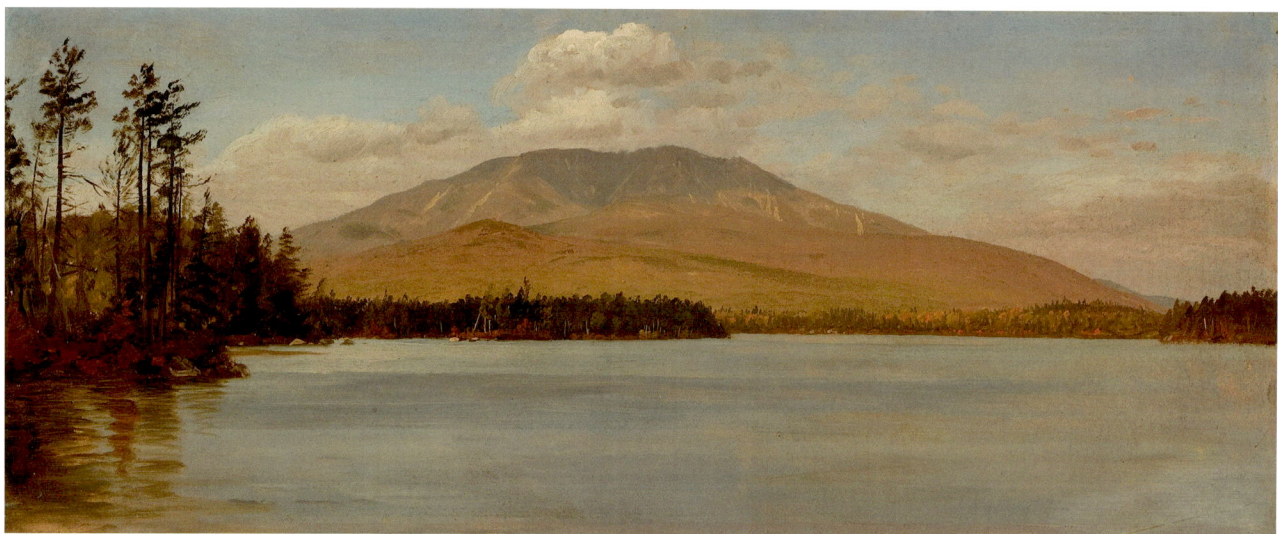

Fig. 60. Frederic Edwin Church, *Mount Katahdin from Upper Togue Lake*,
c. 1877–78, oil on academy board, 8⅛ × 20 in., OL.1981.70

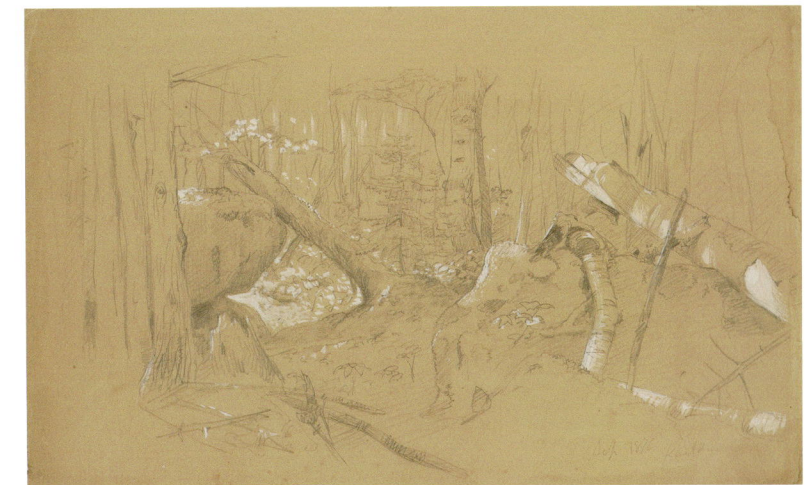

Fig. 61. Frederic Edwin Church, *Forest Interior near Mount Katahdin*, September 1876, graphite and gouache on medium brown paper, 10¾ × 17⅞ in., OL.1977.185

Fig. 62. Frederic Edwin Church, *Wood Interior near Mount Katahdin*, c. 1877, oil on paper mounted on canvas, 12⁵⁄₁₆ × 17¹⁄₁₆ in., OL.1980.1871

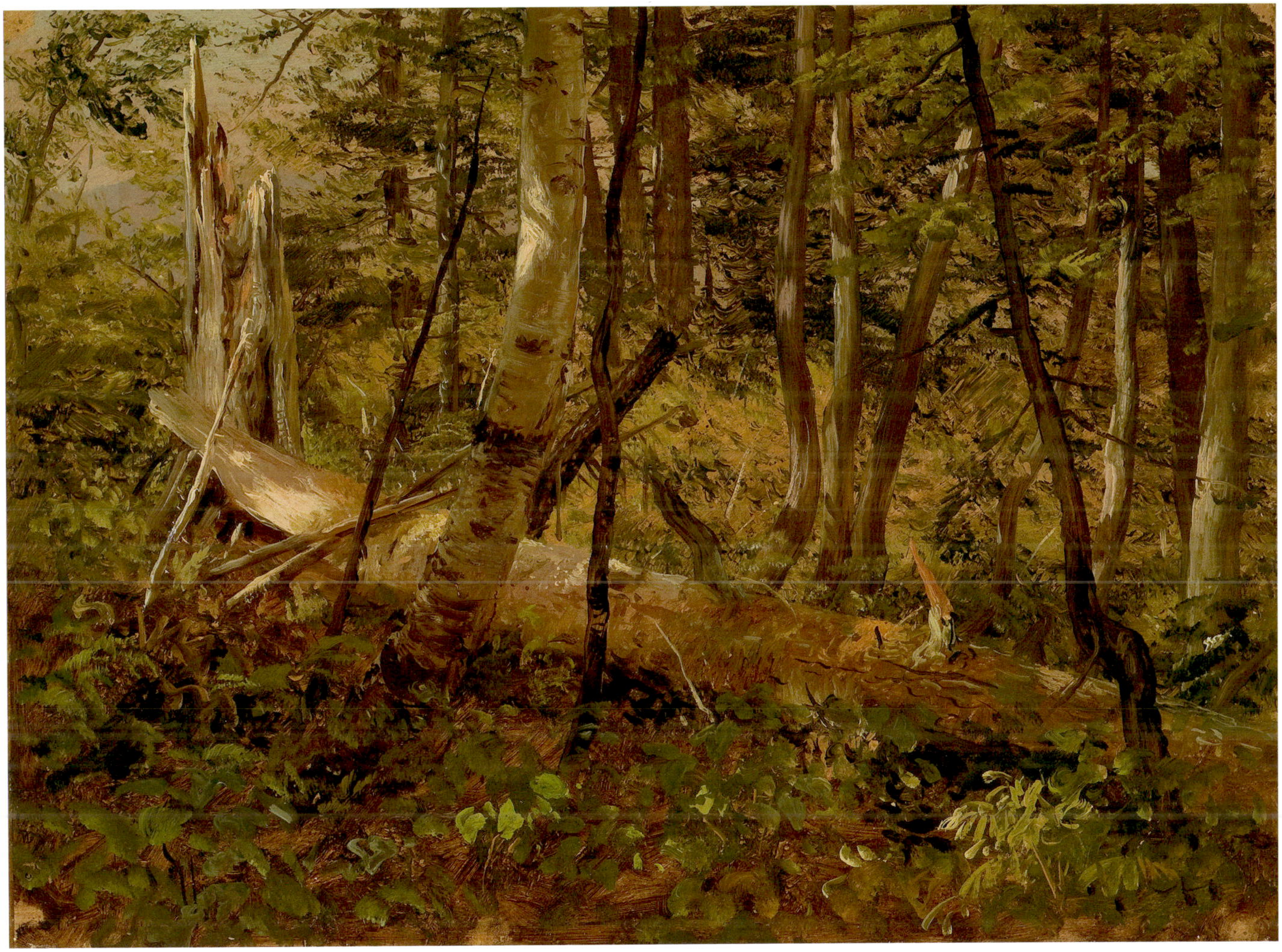

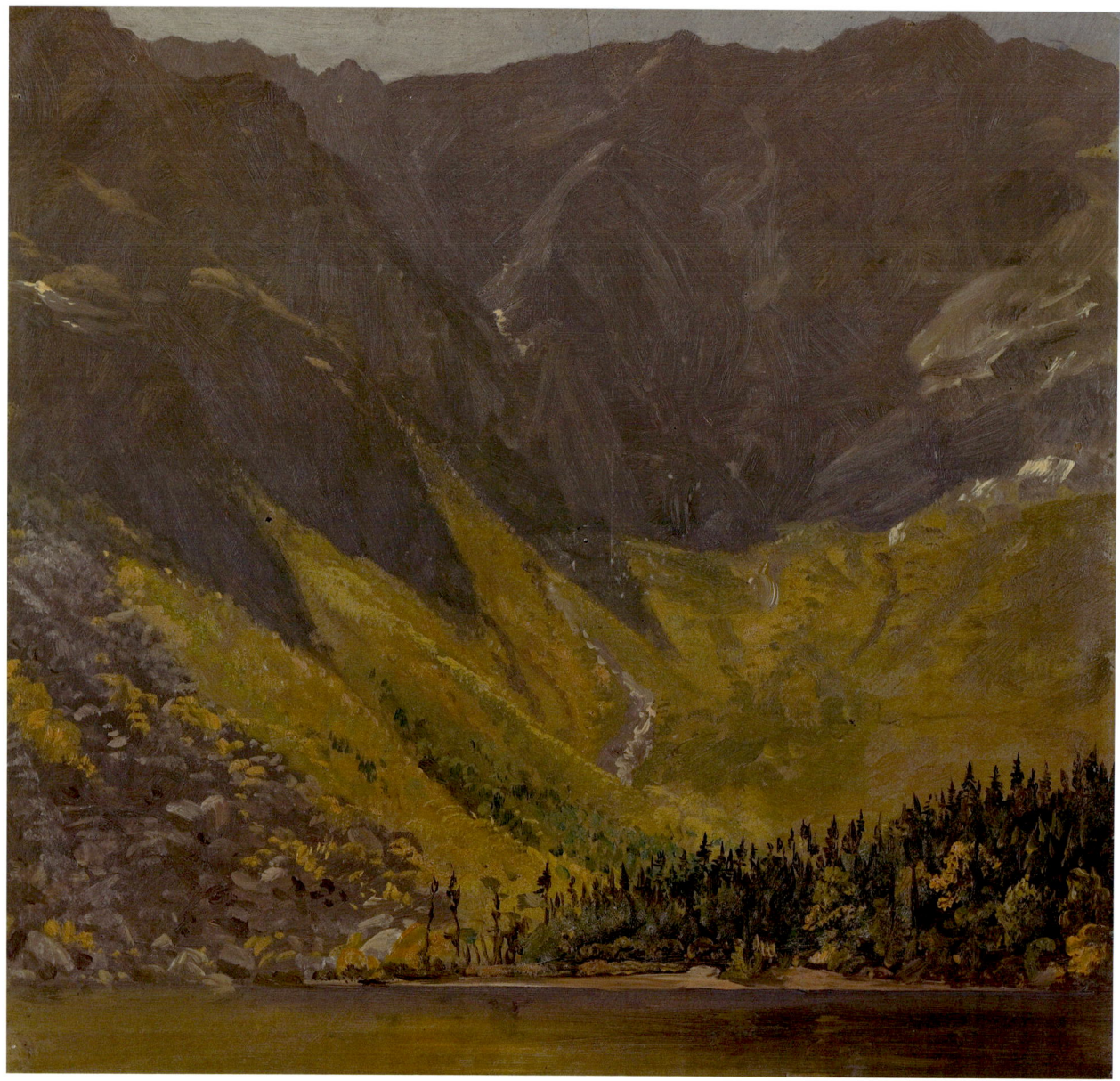

Fig. 63. Frederic Edwin Church, *Great Basin, Mount Katahdin, Maine*, before 1878, oil and traces of graphite on paperboard, 12 × 12¹⁵⁄₁₆ in., Cooper-Hewitt National Design Museum, Smithsonian Institution, New York, Gift of Louis P. Church, 1917-4-632. Photograph: Matt Flynn, Image Courtesy Cooper-Hewitt National Design Museum/Art Resource, NY

Maine Woods in the vicinity of Mt. Ktaadn with your fishing rod. It has a wonderful climate," Church wrote to a friend.[38] Many of these are beautiful and technically precise vignettes, but they seldom led to singular completed projects as they had earlier at Mount Desert. Some of the strongest are of the Great Basin at Katahdin (fig. 63). These tend to be gentle pastoral images, no longer scientifically motivated or emotionally charged (figs. 64 and 65).

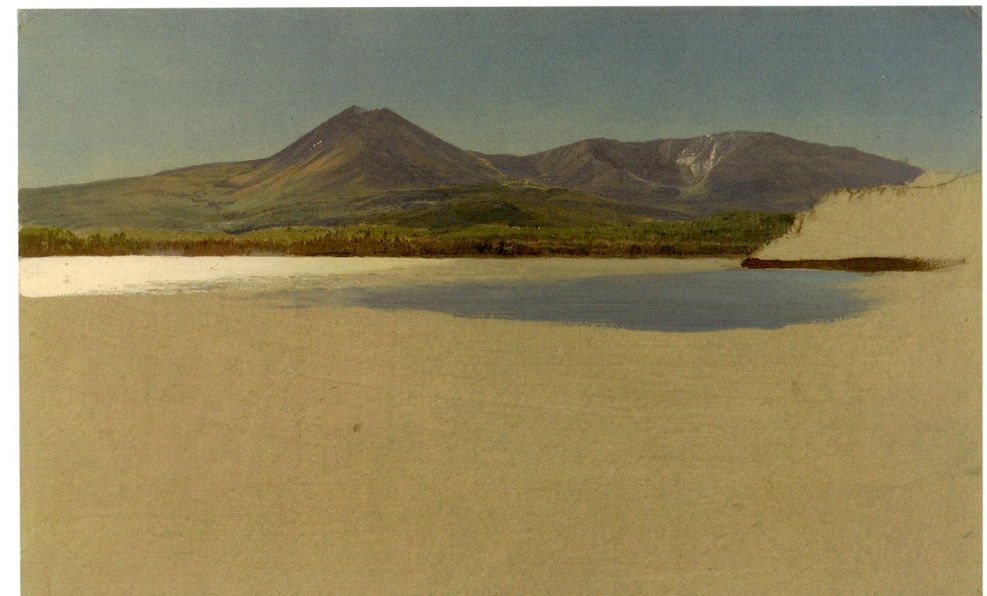

Fig. 64. Frederic Edwin Church, *Mount Katahdin Rising over Katahdin Lake*, before 1878, oil and graphite on paperboard, 12¹⁄₁₆ × 20 in., Cooper-Hewitt National Design Museum, Smithsonian Institution, New York, Gift of Louis P. Church, 1917-4-626. Photograph: Matt Flynn, Image Courtesy Cooper-Hewitt National Design Museum/Art Resource, NY

Fig. 65. Frederic Edwin Church, *Mounts Katahdin and Turner from Lake Katahdin, Maine*, 1855–60, graphite and oil on paperboard, 12¹⁄₁₆ × 20¹⁄₁₆ in., Cooper-Hewitt National Design Museum, Smithsonian Institution, New York, Gift of Louis P. Church, 1917-4-643. Photograph: Matt Flynn, Image Courtesy Cooper-Hewitt National Design Museum/Art Resource, NY

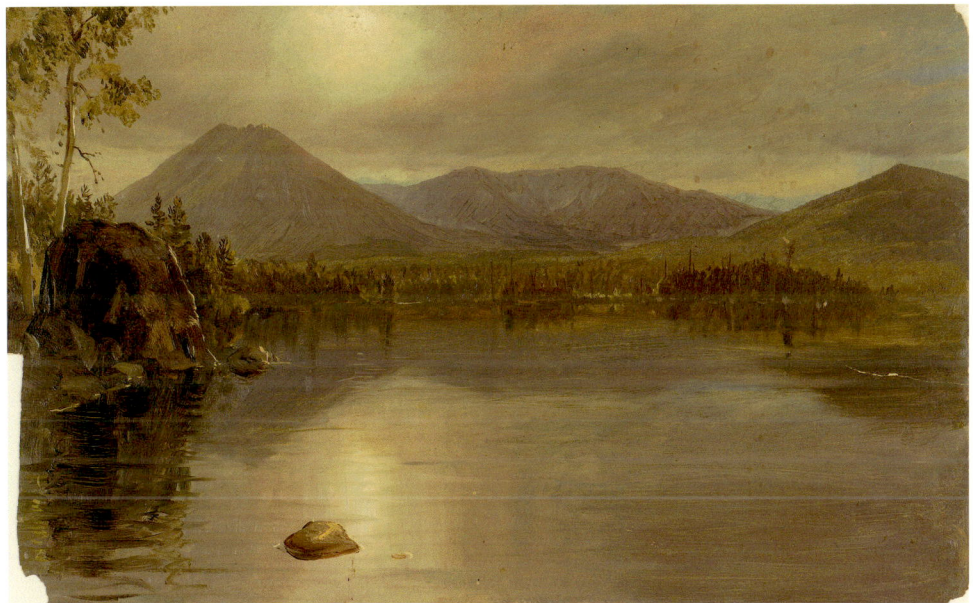

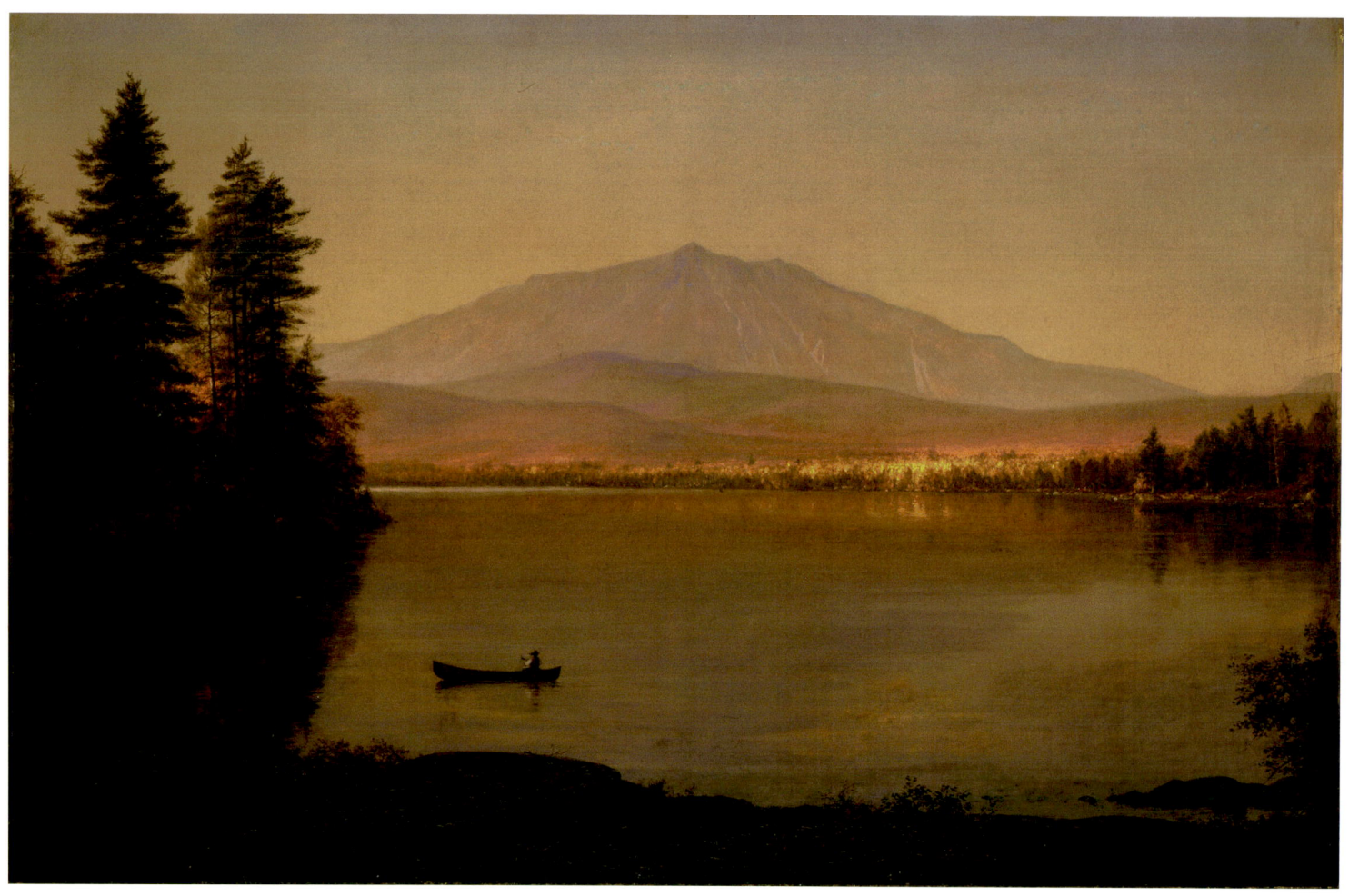

Fig. 66. Frederic Edwin Church, *Mount Katahdin from Millinocket Camp*, 1895, oil on canvas, 26½ × 42¼ in., Portland Museum of Art, Maine, Gift of Owen W. and Anna H. Wells in memory of Elizabeth B. Noyce, 1998.96

After his final visit, Church continued to paint occasional canvases of Mount Katahdin, some of good size. Very different from the visual exultations he recorded on his first visits, these are calm and reflective, often bathed in pink light. The foregrounds are mostly empty and often in shadow, the peak reached across an expanse of flat open water. The mood seems wistful and elegiac. Rather than inviting a fierce climb, these works were a meditation on something enduring at a great distance away. In later years debilitating and painful arthritis made painting ever more difficult. Church's last dated canvas was *Mount Katahdin from Millinocket Camp*, painted in 1895 (fig. 66), which he presented to his wife, Isabel, as a birthday gift. His accompanying note read, "Your old guide is paddling his canoe in the shadow, but he knows that the glories of the heavens and the earth are seen more appreciatively when the observer rests in the shade."[39] He had been painting the great summits of Maine for forty-five years, from 1850 to 1895, expressing the most public and personal themes of his lifetime.

NOTES

1. John Wilmerding, *The Artist's Mount Desert: American Painters on the Maine Coast* (Princeton: Princeton University Press, 1994), chapter II, "The Early Nineteenth Century," pp. 13–25.

2. The Cole sketchbook is now in the Princeton University Art Museum.

3. Wilmerding, *The Artist's Mount Desert*, chapter III, "Thomas Cole," pp. 27–43, documents all the Maine drawings in the Princeton sketchbook along with the resulting canvases.

4. The Achenbach that David Huntington illustrated in the first modern study of Church was *Sunset off a Stormy Coast of Sicily*, 1853 (The Metropolitan Museum of Art), which of course postdated the 1849 Academy exhibition. A more recent Church biographer, John K. Howat, identifies the probable picture exhibited as *Clearing Up, Coast of Sicily*. See David C. Huntington, *The Landscapes of Frederic Edwin Church: Vision of an American Era* (New York: George Braziller, 1966), p. 35, and fig. 61; and John K. Howat, *Frederic Church* (New Haven: Yale University Press, 2005), p. 31.

5. "American Art and Artists," *Bulletin of the American Art-Union*, no. 5 (August 1850), p. 81, quoted in Howat, *Frederic Church*, p. 32. See also Gail Davidson et al., *Frederic Church, Winslow Homer, and Thomas Moran: Tourism and the American Landscape* (New York: Cooper-Hewitt, National Design Museum, 2006), p. 58; Franklin Kelly "A Passion for Landscape: The Paintings of Frederic Edwin Church," in Franklin Kelly et al., *Frederic Edwin Church* (Washington, D.C.: National Gallery of Art, 1989), p. 71, footnote 51; "Art and Artists," *The Home Journal* (February 15, 1851), p. 3.

6. Mary B. Cowdrey and Theodore Sizer, *American Academy of Fine Arts and American Art-Union Exhibition Record, 1816–1852* (New York: New-York Historical Society, 1953), p. 221.

7. For a full account of the history and geology of Mount Desert Island, see Wilmerding, *The Artist's Mount Desert*, chapter I, "The Timeless Place," pp. 3–11.

8. "Mountain Views and Coast Scenery, by a Landscape Painter," *Bulletin of the American Art-Union*, no. 8 (November 1850), pp. 129–31, quoted in Howat, *Frederic Church*, p. 33. Howat notes that the highest summit on the island, Cadillac (originally Green) Mountain, is actually 1,300 feet.

9. Gerald L. Carr, *Frederic Edwin Church: Catalogue Raisonné of Works of Art at Olana State Historic Site*, 2 vols. (New York: Cambridge University Press, 1994), vol. I: p. 182, no. 287, vol. II: no. 287.

10. This last drawing looks northeasterly and is unlikely to be taken from Dorr Mountain, as one would see only a single further hill on the eastern side of the island, Newport Mountain, and then Frenchman's Bay. Here two slopes are clearly evident, one fully modeled and the other outlined. A more plausible location is Jordan Cliffs overlooking Jordan Pond, the Bubbles, and Pemetic beyond.

11. "Mountain Views and Coast Scenery, by a Landscape Painter," p. 130, quoted in Franklin Kelly, *Frederic Edwin Church and the National Landscape* (Washington, D.C.: Smithsonian Institution Press, 1988), p. 36.

12. Henry David Thoreau, *A Week on the Concord and Merrimack Rivers* (New York: Penguin Classics, [1849], 1998), pp. 35, 94.

13. Charles Colbert, *Haunted Visions: Spiritualism and American Art* (Philadelphia: University of Pennsylvania Press, 2011), p. 117.

14. In addition, Charles T. Jackson, the brother-in-law of Thoreau's mentor Ralph Waldo Emerson, had just published his field studies of Maine geology in 1837–39. See Joseph J. Moldenhauer, ed., *Henry David Thoreau: The Illustrated Maine Woods* (Princeton: Princeton University Press, 1974), Introduction, pp. xiii, xv.

15. Ibid., pp. 66, 69.

16. Ralph Waldo Emerson, *The Complete Essays and Other Writings* (New York: Modern Library, 1950), p. 5.

17. Henry David Thoreau, *A Year in Thoreau's Journal: 1851* (New York: Penguin Classics, 1993), (May 25), p. 53, and (September 12), p. 221.

18. Ibid. (February 27), p. 24, (December 12), p. 315, (December 27), p. 321.

19. Alan D. Hodder, *Thoreau's Ecstatic Witness* (New Haven: Yale University Press, 2001), pp. 162–63.

20. Moldenhauer, *The Illustrated Maine Woods*, p. 64. See also Hodder, *Thoreau's Ecstatic Witness*, p. 123.

21. Moldenhauer, *The Illustrated Maine Woods*, p. 71.

22. Howat, *Frederic Church*, p. 63, quoting *The Crayon* (April 11, 1855), p. 234.

23. Wilmerding, *The Artist's Mount Desert*, chapter VII, "The Late Nineteenth Century," pp. 125–55.

24. Anne Mazlish, ed., *The Tracy Log Book, 1855, A Month in Summer* (Bar Harbor, Maine: Acadia Publishing Company, 1977), pp. 57, 61.

25. Ibid., pp. 61–62, 69, 80, 127, 135.

26. Howat, *Frederic Church*, p. 64, quoting Laura Winthrop Johnson, sister of Theodore Winthrop.

27. Ibid., pp. 65–67, from Theodore Winthrop, *Life in the Open Air, and Other Papers* (Boston: Ticknor and Fields, 1863), pp. 50, 104, 114.

28. For example, *A Country Home*, 1854 (Seattle Art Museum), *Twilight (Sunset)*, 1856 (Albany Institute of History and Art), and *Twilight (Catskill Mountain)*, 1856–58 (private collection).

29. Huntington, *The Landscapes of Frederic Edwin Church*, pp. 81–82.

30. Kelly, *Frederic Edwin Church and the National Landscape*, pp. 117–18. Chapter 7 is wholly dedicated to outlining the process and reception of the painting. See also Kelly et al., *Frederic Edwin Church*, p. 59.

31. Howat, *Frederic Church*, p. 100. The most recent consideration of this and related paintings during the war period is Kevin J. Avery, "Rally 'Round the Flag: Frederic Edwin Church and the Civil War," *Antiques & Fine Art*, vol. 11, no. 1 (Spring 2011), pp. 208–13; and his longer article of the same title in *The Hudson River Valley Review*, vol. 27, no. 2 (Spring 2011), pp. 66–103. In addition, the Smithsonian American Art Museum and The Metropolitan Museum of Art are planning a full survey exhibition in 2012 of American art in the context of the Civil War.

32. Thanks to R. Alexander Boyle for information about the spectacular eruption of northern lights in August–September 1859, and the commentary in newspapers across America and Europe during the first days of September.

33. This sequence of works is discussed in Avery, "Rally 'Round the Flag," *Antiques & Fine Art*, pp. 209–10.

34. For many years this was misleadingly titled *Sunrise off the Maine Coast* but could not have looked east, given the relationship of rocky coast and water in this composition.

35. A. L. Holley, "Camps and Tramps about Ktaadn," *Scribner's Monthly*, vol. 16 (May 1878), pp. 33–47. The original offprint from the *Scribner's* article is in the Olana archives, OL.2000.438. The article began with an engraving drawn by Thomas Moran and engraved by F. S. King after a study of Katahdin by Church. See Howat, *Frederic Church*, p. 173 (see frontispiece).

36. Davidson, *Frederic Church, Winslow Homer, and Thomas Moran*, p. 65.

37. Holley, *Camps and Tramps*, p. 36. Quoted in Howat, *Frederic Church*, p. 173.

38. Frederic Church to A. C. Goodman, October 3, 1885, OL.1983.1463. Quoted in Howat, *Frederic Church*, p. 173.

39. Frederic Church to Isabel Church, November 10, 1895, OL.1985.18. Quoted in ibid., p. 182.

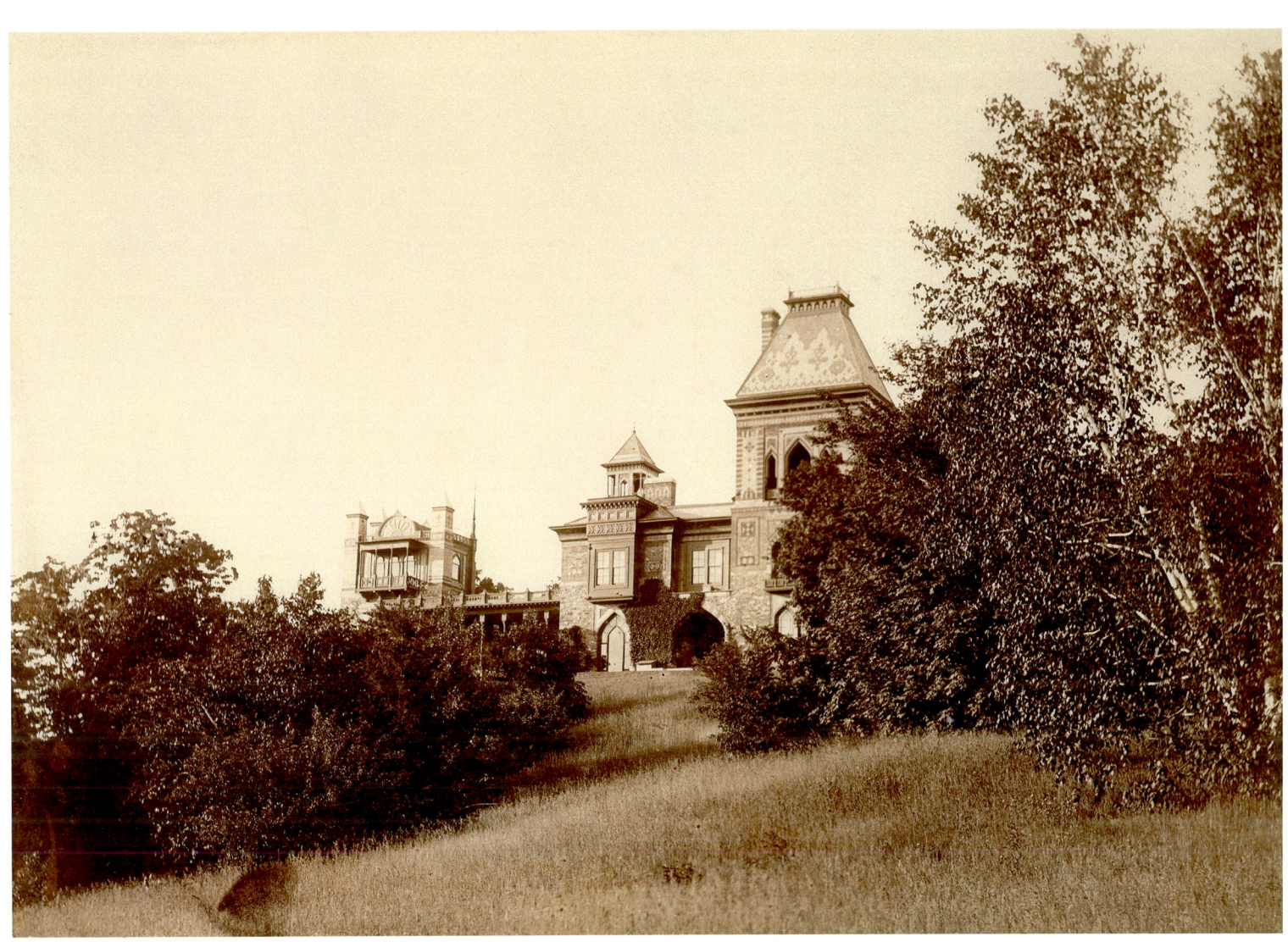

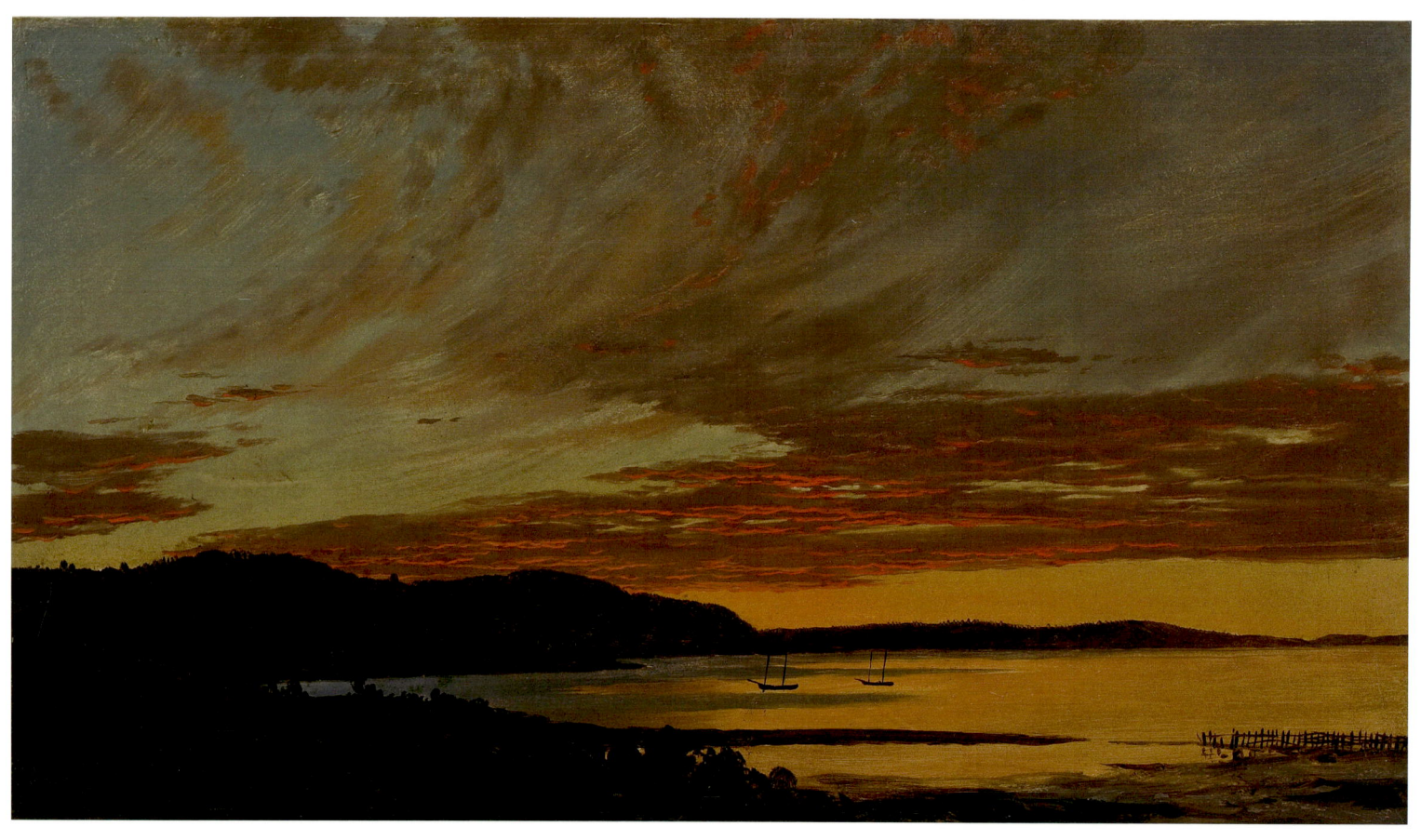

*Maine Sublime: Frederic Edwin Church's Landscapes
of Mount Desert and Mount Katahdin*

EXHIBITION VENUES
Portland Museum of Art, Maine
June 30–September 30, 2012

The Evelyn and Maurice Sharp Gallery
Olana State Historic Site, Hudson, New York
June 29–October 27, 2013

The Cleveland Museum of Art
October 4, 2014–January 25, 2015

Works in the Exhibition from the Olana Collection

The following works appear in the order that they are presented in the book. All works are by Frederic Edwin Church.

Granite Cliffs, Mount Desert Island, c. August 1850, graphite on light brown paper, 10¹³⁄₁₆ × 15 in., OL.1977.112 (fig. 9)

Cliffs and Rocky Cove, Mount Desert Island, c. August 1850, oil on light brown cardboard, 12⅛ × 16⅛ in., OL.1978.22 (fig. 10)

Rock Outcropping, Mount Desert Island, August 1850, graphite and gouache on coarse light brown paper, 11³⁄₁₆ × 12⅜ in., OL.1980.1445 (fig. 13)

Stone Pillar, Mount Desert Island, September 2, 1850, graphite on coarse light brown paper, 11¼ × 14½ in., OL.1980.1450 recto (fig. 14)

Evergreen Trees, Mount Desert Island, c. August 1850, graphite and gouache on coarse light brown paper, 14⅝ × 11¼ in., OL.1980.1990 (fig. 16)

Birch Tree Struck by Lightning, Mount Desert Island, August 1850, graphite and gouache on coarse light brown paper, 11¹³⁄₁₆ × 14⁹⁄₁₆ in., OL.1980.1442 (fig. 17)

Peninsula in Somes Sound, Mount Desert Island, c. July–August 1850, graphite and gouache on coarse brown paper, 7⅝ × 11¼ in., OL.1980.1507 (fig. 19)

Monument Rock, Mount Desert Island, c. August 1850, graphite and gouache on light brown paper, 11⅝ × 15⅝ in., OL.1977.116 verso (fig. 20)

Lumber Mill, Mount Desert Island, c. July–August 1850, graphite, gouache, and chalk on gray-green paper, 10¼ × 15 in., OL.1980.1610 (fig. 23)

Mount Desert Island from near Sullivan, September 1854, graphite, gouache, and white lead on gray-green paper, 10¾ × 17⁵⁄₁₆ in., OL.1980.1459 (fig. 36)

Mount Desert Island, c. 1855–56, graphite and gouache on light brown paper, 9³⁄₁₆ × 15 in., OL1980.1989 recto (fig. 37)

Sunset, Bar Harbor, September 1854, graphite on tan paper, 9¹¹⁄₁₆ × 16¹³⁄₁₆ in., OL.1980.1448 (fig. 38)

Sunset, Bar Harbor, c. September 1854, oil on paper mounted on canvas, 10⅛ × 17¼ in., OL.1981.72 (fig. 39)

Maine Sunset, c. 1856, oil on paper mounted on canvas, 10 × 17½ in., OL.1980.1889 (fig. 41)

Maine Twilight, c. 1856, oil on heavy buff paper, 11⁷⁄₁₆ × 17⁹⁄₁₆ in., OL.1978.12 (fig. 42)

Sunset, c. 1856–65, oil on paper mounted on ragboard and panel, 11⅝ × 18¼ in., OL.1980.1633 (fig. 43)

Twilight, A Sketch, 1858, oil on canvas, 8¼ × 12¼ in., OL.1981.8 (fig. 45)

Frederic and Isabel Church at Mount Desert Island, c. 1860–62, graphite on thin white wove paper, 8 × 5 in., OL.1980.1603 (fig. 53)

Wood Interior on Mount Turner, c. 1877, oil and graphite on paper mounted on canvas, 12⁵⁄₁₆ × 20⁵⁄₁₆ in., OL.1980.1869 (fig. 58)

Campfire near Mount Katahdin, c. 1877, oil on paper mounted on canvas, 12⅜ × 20⅜ in., OL.1980.1916 (fig. 59)

Mount Katahdin from Upper Togue Lake, c. 1877–78, oil on academy board, 8⅛ × 20 in., OL.1981.70 (fig. 60)

Forest Interior near Mount Katahdin, September 1876, graphite and gouache on medium brown paper, 10¾ × 17⅞ in., OL.1977.185 (fig. 61)

Wood Interior near Mount Katahdin, c. 1877, oil on paper mounted on canvas, 12⁵⁄₁₆ × 17¹⁄₁₆ in., OL.1980.1871 (fig. 62)

The organizers of *Maine Sublime: Frederic Edwin Church's Landscapes of Mount Desert and Mount Katahdin* wish to acknowledge the generous early support received from

    Susan Winokur and Paul Leach
    The Peter Jay Sharp Foundation

This book and the accompanying exhibition were made possible by major grants from

    The Mr. and Mrs. Raymond J. Horowitz Foundation for
        the Arts, Inc.
    The New York State Council on the Arts Museum Program
    The Wyeth Foundation for American Art

Additional support has been provided by

    Valerie and Brock Ganeles
    Mark LaSalle
    The Olana Exhibition Fund
    The Olana Partnership's Jack Warner Fund
        for Creativity and Innovation
    Gary Schiro and Robert Burns
    Evelyn D. Trebilcock and Douglas Hammond
    Barrie A. and Deedee Wigmore
    John Wilmerding
    Eli Wilner & Co., NYC

We are particularly grateful to Henry and Sharon Martin for their commitment and dedication to supporting the development of high-quality catalogues in conjunction with Olana exhibitions.

Support for John Wilmerding's lectures in conjunction with the exhibition at each venue was provided by CHRISTIE'S.

The Trustees and staff of The Olana Partnership wish to recognize the support of Governor Andrew Cuomo; New York State Office of Parks, Recreation and Historic Preservation Commissioner Rose Harvey; Deputy Commissioner for Historic Preservation Ruth Pierpont; Regional Director, Taconic Region, Linda Cooper; Director of the Bureau of Historic Sites John Lovell; former Olana Site Manager Linda McLean, and Olana Site Manager Kimberly Flook.

The Olana Partnership's Jack Warner Fund for Creativity and Innovation was established in December 2009 to honor the work of Jonathan Westervelt Warner. Donations to the Fund are used to enhance Olana exhibitions. We are grateful to the many donors who made gifts to establish this fund in Jack's honor and invite you to consider making a gift.

The Evelyn and Maurice Sharp Gallery was made possible through a generous gift from Richard T. Sharp and is named in memory of his parents. Additional support was provided by Susan Winokur and Paul Leach and by The Peter Jay Sharp Foundation.

Maine Sublime: Frederic Edwin Church's Landscapes of Mount Desert and Mount Katahdin is the fifth annual exhibition in the Evelyn and Maurice Sharp Gallery at Olana. The Olana Partnership, Hudson, New York, and New York State's Office of Parks, Recreation and Historic Preservation, Albany, organized the exhibition. These two institutions are working together to preserve and restore Olana.

Olana

The eminent Hudson River School Painter Frederic Edwin Church (1826–1900) designed Olana, his family home, studio, and estate, as an integrated environment embracing architecture, art, and landscape. Considered one the most important artistic residences in the United States, Olana is a landmark of Picturesque landscape gardening with a Persian-inspired house at its summit, embracing unrivaled panoramic views of the Hudson Valley.

Supporting Olana and The Olana Partnership

The Olana Partnership was founded in 1971 to assist and support New York State in the conservation, preservation, development, and improvement of Olana State Historic Site, which is open to the public throughout the year. We rely on a large number of supporters—individuals, foundations, companies, and public sector sources—to fund our work for the enhancement of Olana and its integral viewshed, to sponsor educational programs, and to foster scholarly research on the artist and his property. This support is essential to sustain Olana's education, outreach, and public programs, to care for the collection, and to support lending from and exhibitions of the collection. Your donation will make a real difference and enable others to enjoy Olana both now and into the future. For more information on how you can help, please contact the Development Office, The Olana Partnership, PO Box 199, Hudson, NY 12534, (518) 828-1872, top@olana.org or visit us at *www.olana.org*.

Our Mission

The Olana Partnership serves to inspire the public by preserving and interpreting Olana, Frederic Edwin Church's artistic masterpiece.

Our Vision

The fully restored Olana, vibrant with the activity of students, visitors, and scholars, will be the most widely recognized artist's home and studio in the world.

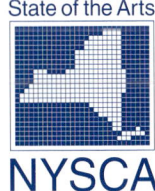

State of the Arts

NYSCA

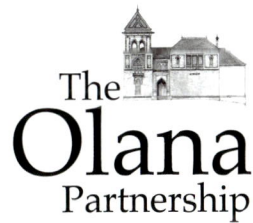

The
Olana
Partnership

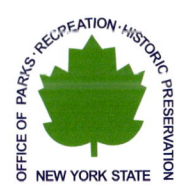

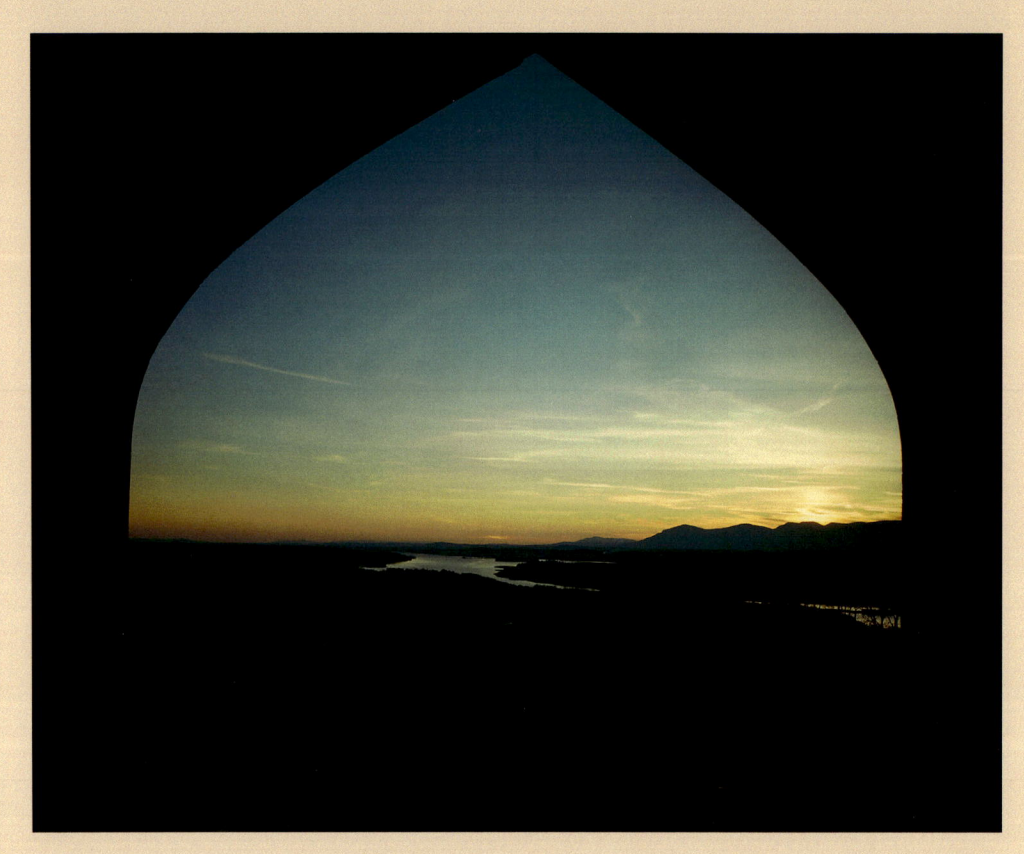